With thanks for your
advice & good
wishes.

[signature]

May 1980.

Rare and Interesting Commercial Vehicles

Rare and Interesting Commercial Vehicles

BY

DAPHNE BAMPTON

MELKSHAM
COLIN VENTON
WHITE HORSE LIBRARY

LIST OF CONTENTS

PLATE 1—1905 Milnes-Daimler Double-Deck Omnibus after restoration (Frontispiece)

LIST OF ILLUSTRATIONS

To my dear husband.

ACKNOWLEDGEMENTS

I wish to thank the many people mentioned in the text who own — or have owned — the commercial vehicles described, particularly Mr James Leake of the United States who has patiently provided much written information. I am grateful for the helpful expertise of Prince Marshall and Nick Baldwin, joint editors of *Old Motor*, Pat Kennet editor of *Truck*, and Mr A. M. Sedgley, General Manager of Southdown Motor Services Limited.

The Public Relations Officers of several vehicle manufacturers have helped me, as have the Officers of Fire and Ambulance Services. I am also grateful for permission to quote extracts from the publications named in the text.

The assistance given by the Reference and Lending Departments of the Swindon Divisional Library has been invaluable. Thanks are also due to Mrs Lorraine Hughes who typed the MS, to Miss Molly Hope who read it and to Mr Edwin Bampton who gave technical advice.

I am indebted to many other people and regret that it is not possible to thank them all by name here.

FOREWORD

Within the span of 70 years the development of commercial road transport has created a world of mobility for everyone. The speedy delivery of goods over large areas and the advent of the motor bus have made an impact on almost every aspect of life. So too has the growth of public services such as ambulance and fire-fighting. Indeed, the amelioration of suffering that results from present-day ambulance services is a good example.

As late as 1900, persons injured on the streets were taken to hospital in horse-drawn cabs or carts — if they were lucky; others were carried on police litters (usually two poles and a piece of cloth), or were conveyed on foot with the support of friends and bystanders. Few, if any, reached hospital without aggravating their condition and some never arrived.

Clearly, the advances made by commercial motor vehicles are too many and too varied to be detailed here. Suffice to say that I have found it an enlightening experience to compile the biographies of several different types of commercial vehicles — all having survived from the great formative years of the industry.

The histories of 20 vehicles covering a cross section of commercial activity are chronicled in the following pages. In each instance factual details of the vehicle are given, as well as information about the manufacturer when this will highlight the social history of the period. Regrettably, it has not been possible

Foreword

to include all the vehicles that I researched because of insufficient data. Where vehicles are included whose biographies contain a few 'missing years' it is because either the vehicle, or the manufacturer, had a noteable role in the commercial road transport industry.

This is a book for the general reader — for the man or woman who will be interested to learn about rare commercial vehicles that were at work at some stage during the years from 1903 to 1936 and still survive in good condition today.

Chapter One

1905 Milnes-Daimler Double-Deck Omnibus.
A new Concept in its day.

This magnificent 1905 Milnes-Daimler bus is believed to be the oldest restored double-decker in the world. It comes from a time when the concept of the motor bus as a practical form of commercial passenger carrying transport was just emerging, and it bears the name of a firm that had a major role in the evolution of this industry.

The Milnes-Daimler Company came into being following an agreement between G. F. Milnes & Co. Ltd., British manufacturers of electric tramcars, and the German Daimler Company. It was established in London in 1902, and within a few months a Milnes-Daimler single-deck bus was on the market. This, however, was only the beginning. The directors of the Company believed that real progress in the embryo bus industry would only come when a practical double-decker could be produced, and early in 1904 they brought out the Milnes-Daimler 34-seater double-deck omnibus. This vehicle was the first efficient double-decker to be designed specifically for the purpose. It was not built on a lorry chassis; neither was it an adaptation of a horse-bus. The Milnes-Daimler was a true double-deck bus, and when it was launched at the Crystal Palace Motor Show early in 1904 it was acknowledged to be an important innovation in the development of omnibus transport.

PLATE 2—1905 Milnes-Daimler Double-Deck Omnibus–
interior before restoration. (As it was in the field when
first seen by James Leake)

PLATE 3—1905 Milnes-Daimler Double-Deck Omnibus—driver's
compartment before restoration
Owner: James Leake

1905 Milnes-Daimler Double-Deck Omnibus

In 1904 there were less than 20 motorised buses at work in London, and only a few in the provinces including those belonging to the forward-looking Great Western Railway Bus Service. Yet, it was obvious that the day of the horse-bus was coming to an end — even if some people could not see it. Others, of course, did not want to see it, and complaints about the smell, the noise, and the dangers of motor buses were many and persistent. The operators' timetables were erratic, and this might also have given cause for complaint if passengers had expected omnibuses to run to time; but they evidently had no such expectations, and an example of this appears in 'The Southdown Story' (published by Southdown Motor Services Limited) in connection with vehicles owned by the Sussex Motor Road Car Company in 1904:

"..... If the bus that should have reached Pulborough at 5.30 p.m. ambled in at about 7.00 p.m. it was considered by all concerned to be a pretty good effort."

Despite its imperfections the motor bus industry grew throughout 1904, and go-ahead commercial concerns began to grasp the importance of this form of transport. For instance, a newspaper advertisement appearing in 1905 for the George Hotel, Trowbridge, Wiltshire, stated in heavy print that the hotel's "Motor bus meets trains". The availability of a motor bus was always given prominence in hotel advertising of the period, and seemed to be accorded the same level of importance as the provision of "A Bath".

By 1905 the motor bus industry was established beyond recall, between 200 and 300 vehicles were in service in London and numbers had grown correspondingly in other parts of the country. Much of the credit for this progress is accorded to the Milnes-Daimler double-decker. The vehicle was practical, economic, and reasonably reliable; and prominent horse-bus operators, such as Thomas Tilling and Birch Brothers, were quick to recognise its advantages. Both companies had Milnes-Daimler double-deckers running in London by the beginning of 1905 — two being in service with Birch Brothers and three in Tilling livery.

Other bus companies were soon buying Milnes-Daimler double-deckers, among them the London General Omnibus Company and the London Motor Omnibus Company. The make was also popular in the provinces, and the vehicle of this chapter was purchased new in May 1905 by the Tunbridge Wells, Southborough & District Omnibus Company. It was registered D1959 on the 26th of that month.**

As with all 'beginnings' the early years of the motorised buses were vigorous, yet fraught with difficulties. Many companies were formed and many failed, or at best faltered. The Tunbridge Wells, Southborough & District was such a one, and having purchased D1959 in May 1905, it was obliged to sell the vehicle in August of the same year in an effort to overcome its financial difficulties. Another Milnes-Daimler double-decker in the Company's fleet (D1642) was offered for sale at the same time, and both buses were bought by the Brighton, Hove & Preston United Omnibus Company.

The Brighton, Hove & Preston United Omnibus Company had been established as a horse-bus operation in 1884. It was one of the early companies to put motor buses into service and was considerably more substantial than the first owner of the Milnes-Daimlers. Furthermore, BH&P had the facilities

** Information supplied by Old Motor magazine.

necessary to keep its buses in good order, and the two double-deckers remained in the Company's fleet until 1915 — but not in its livery. Having been painted by their first owner they could not be adapted to the BH&P livery of polished mahogany, and the Company painted them deep purple lake. Thus distinguished, the two buses became well known to residents in the Brighton district who nicknamed them 'the little chocolate boxes'.

During the time that D1959 was in service with the Brighton, Hove & Preston United Omnibus Company it was off the road for major alterations on two occasions. The first occured in 1907 when the vehicle was converted to chain drive. This conversion was made on many Milnes-Daimlers of the period because the original rack and pinion drive was noisy. In 1910 the vehicle was called in for a thorough overhaul and was fitted with the body of another bus in the BH&P fleet.

Thereafter it returned to service, and was still on the road in 1914 when BH&P, like other omnibus operators, began to feel the effects of World War I. Problems arose because military sources were using their powers to requisition the bus companies' best vehicles at a time when the demand for public transport was accelerating rapidly. It was as a result of these difficulties that the Brighton, Hove & Preston United Omnibus Company joined with other bus operators to pool their resources and form Southdown Motor Services Limited. This new undertaking was incorporated on 2nd June, 1915, and was to go on to become one of the most important bus operations in the South of England.

Certainly, the new Company made an efficient start, and by July its official timetable was on sale at ½d per copy. This document contained a number of regulations that sound strange today, and the following extracts have been taken from 'The Southdown Story':

> "Passengers are requested to hail the driver when they wish the omnibus to stop for them to enter, and not the conductor.

> "Ladies are not allowed to travel on the front seat unless accompanied by a gentleman.

> "Small dogs may be carried at owner's risk if they are clean and are not a nuisance or cause inconvenience to the passengers, and provided there is sufficient accommodation to carry them conveniently. But the Company reserve the right to refuse to carry any dog. Under no circumstances will passengers' dogs be allowed to run with the bus."

Southdown Motor Services owned a number of Milnes-Daimlers when it was set-up, and records of the Company show that several more were acquired within a few months. The Milnes-Daimler double-decker of this chapter became part of the Southdown fleet at the time of the merger in 1915; but it had already been at work for ten years and the Company disposed of it in 1917.

Definite evidence of the vehicle's whereabouts after it left the Southdown fleet has been difficult to find but the present owner has information to indicate that the old bus went to the Continent and "spent its days during the remainder of the Great War hauling troops about in Holland and France". It is thought that it returned to England after the War and was then in use for a short period.

Thereafter the old double-decker disappeared from sight and knowledge. No records of its whereabouts have been found, and it was next heard of in the 1960's when Jeremy Bacon saw it in use as a caravan by the Thames at Hampton Court. He recognised the

PLATE 4—1905 Milnes-Daimler Double-Deck Omnibus—carburettor side of engine before restoration. (Note the open inlet valve gear)

Owner: James Leake

PLATE 5—1905 Milnes-Daimler Double-Deck Omnibus viewed from rear end before restoration

Owner: James Leake

historic significance of the vehicle and was able to purchase it without too much delay. It was Mr Bacon's intention to restore the Milnes-Daimler — but there was never time, and in the late 1960's the vehicle was in the hands of Mr P. Foulkes-Halbard.

This was when Mr James Leake of Muskogee, Oklahoma, U.S.A., heard of the ancient double-decker, and he still has pleasant recollections of the afternoon in 1969 when, in company with his wife and Mr Ted Woolley, he visited P. Foulkes-Halbard and purchased the vehicle. He especially remembers Mr Foulkes-Halbard's lively little donkey which began to bray as soon as he heard the clink of the visitors' tea-cups and would not stop until he too was given his tea, or in his case — his oats.

James Leake is the owner of one of the finest antique car museums in the States and his experience of vintage vehicles is extensive. He is a regular visitor to Britain and has attended several London to Brighton Veteran Car Runs. When I met him he spoke with enthusiasm of his splendid old Milnes-Daimler bus, and while describing his first sight of the vehicle he said: "It was standing in a field with grass growing up through the spark plug holes and pieces of mechanism strewn around". Naturally, Mr Leake feared that the 1905 double-decker might be beyond restoration, but from the beginning he decided that if it could be restored it would be well done. In the event the Milnes-Daimler was restored to first-class condition, although five years passed before it reached this desirable state.

The restoration was work for craftsmen, and some time elapsed before James Leake could arrange for it to be done. When he was, at last, able to spend several weeks in this country he discussed the project with Mr Prince Marshall of Old Motor magazine, and

plans were then made for the restoration to be undertaken by highly skilled coachbuilders and engineers.
Mr Leake explained in a recent letter that "many parts
had to be re-manufactured, including chains for the
drive chain, timing gears and pistons". He added that
Dunlop Holdings Limited made a special project to re-
build the tyres on the chassis.

As it happened that James Leake was able to make
only brief visits to Britain during the re-building, he
was pleased that the work was supervised by Mr
Leonard Potter of Kintbury and Mr H. F. Fergusson-
Wood who is a former director of Jack Barclays
(Service) Limited. Both men are well known for their
knowledge of vintage vehicles. In fact, much expertise
and many people were involved in the restoration of
this notable double-decker.

The bus has been restored to its 1907 condition, that
is *after* the Milnes-Daimler rack and pinion drive had
been replaced with chain drive, and *before* the original
body was replaced with the body of another bus. It
still bears the registration number D1959 and has been
painted and signwritten to re-create its original
appearance. So, with the exception of chain drive, this
1905 double decker is the same today as it was 70 years
ago when the residents of Brighton christened it 'the
little chocolate box'.

Mr Leake believes that elderly vehicles should be
driven — even those in their seventies — and when the
Milnes-Daimler was restored it was entered for the
1976 Historic Commercial Vehicle Club's London to
Brighton Run. Since this was almost certainly the
double decker's first major outing for 60 years it was
essential to have an experienced driver, and Tim
Nicholson, who is an authority on vintage commercial
vehicles, agreed to undertake the trip. In a letter
written from America after the London/Brighton James

Leake said that Mr Nicholson did "a masterful job in tuning the bus, getting it going and driving it".
getting it going and driving it".

Undoubtedly, the vehicle is 'different' when it comes to driving, and mention of just a few of the peculiarities of its construction will show how great the difference is. For instance, the hand brake, which operates on both rear wheels, consists of contracting bands lined with woven friction material, while the foot brake is a transmission brake comprised of a single brake drum on the end of the output shaft of the gearbox. The only foot pedal is situated on the left of the steering column, and operates both the clutch and the foot brake, with the result that it must first disengage the clutch before final pressure will apply the brake. Therefore, when the driver applies the foot brake he has no help from retardation of the engine and is likely to use the hand brake on downhill stretches.

Other strange characteristics include three gear-change levers: one lever operates 1st/2nd gears, another 3rd/4th, and the third lever is for reverse. The vehicle does not have a foot accelerator, instead there is a long lever for hand operation to the left of the steering column.

It is not surprising that in a letter to *Old Motor* [*Vol 9 No 5*] Tim Nicholson described the drive from Battersea to Brighton as the"experience of a lifetime". Just one paragraph is sufficient to show how singularly 'different' is the driving technique required:

"When the right hand is not engaged in keeping the vehicle on the straight and narrow via an extremely small steering wheel, or checking the speed with the handbrake, it can be used in adjusting the mixture control lever mounted on the right hand side of the dash. Also, when the left hand is not used for controlling the throttle lever to extract the maximum from the engine, or for changing gear, or for assisting the right hand in performing a steering manoeuvre, it can be used at periodic intervals to operate the engine oil pump. There is nothing whatsoever for the right foot to do.''

Despite these odd features Mr Nicholson achieved a reasonably trouble-free drive, and he reached Brighton in just over six hours — a journey of about 53 miles. In his own words progress was ''slow'' but uneventful.

The fact that D1959 can travel so uneventfully on today's crowded roads is a tribute to all those who were involved in its restoration, and James Leake was anxious that people in Britain should have the opportunity to see the restored vehicle. For this reason he intended to leave it on display at the National Motor Museum at Beaulieu for a year or two, and he was disappointed when H. M. Customs and Excise announced that Value Added Tax must be paid on the restoration if the vehicle remained in Britain — even temporarily. That the British public would wish to see a unique 70-year-old bus that had been built in this country and restored here did not signify. The demand for V.A.T. was not waived, and the aged double-decker was shipped to the States shortly after the 1976 London to Brighton Run.

Mr Leake is still sorry that his Milnes-Daimler could not be exhibited in Britain, and he expressed this in a letter when he said: ''I would have liked to have shown the vehicle in England for several years so that everyone could have the pleasure of admiring such a beautiful restoration''.

Today, this 1905 double-decker is a notable attraction in the Leake Antique Car Museum in Muskogee and — what is more — it can sometimes be seen in action. James Leake wrote in 1978 saying that it had just been driven to a celebration staged for the opening of a new factory in his district. Directors of the new company

Plate 6—1905 Milnes-Daimler Double-Deck Omnibus with driver and conductor. Taken while in service with the Brighton, Hove & Preston United Omnibus Company in Brighton circa 1912

Plate 7—1913 Model T Ford Rural Bus

Owner and Photo: Henry Wyatt

with members of the local Chamber of Commerce were passengers on the bus, and Mr Leake was at the wheel. He described the vehicle's performance thus:

> "The bus has a top speed of just fifteen miles downhill. The little engine purrs like a watch, but will pick up a gradient faster than a surveyor's instrument will. One forgets how really primitive this machine is, and it is perhaps the most primitive of any I have. It has open timing gears, open valves, and T-head engine. The transmission is larger than the engine. I imagine it takes more energy to work the transmission than it does to move the whole bus. It is chain drive."

The known history of this splendid old omnibus was extended during March 1978 when James Leake received a letter from Norah Horton of Burnley, Lancashire. Miss Horton had heard about the bus and she wrote to say that her father was the architect who drew up the plans for the original body. Mr Leake was delighted with this information, and he was excited to receive the original blueprint shortly afterwards.

The details of this 73-year-old blueprint are as set out below:

TOP SEAT MOTOR OMNIBUS
Scale one inch to one foot.
Seating Capacity 36.
Passengers inside 16
Passengers on roof 18.
Passengers on driver's seat 2.

General Dimensions	ft.	ins.
Length over corner pillars	12	8
Length of compartment inside	10	8
Length of driver's canopy	4	0
Length of entrance platform	2	10
Width over roof	6	3

21

Width over pillars	5	9
Width of doorway	2	3
Height of doorway	5	10
Height inside at centre — floor to ceiling	6	1
Wheel base of chassis	11	8¼

Drawing No. H 5215   22.3.05.

Clearly, D1959 is historically important. It is a perfect example of the motorised bus at the moment when it emerged as a practical form of commercial passenger carrying transport. In addition it is a Milnes-Daimler double-decker and, as such, it had a pioneering role in the development of the industry.

It is pleasant to know that this admirably restored vehicle now reflects human enterprise and skill in two very different periods of history.

Chapter Two

1913 Model T Ford Rural Bus
Of Diverse Abilities

By 1913 Ford Model T Cars were selling well in Britain and the Model T 'Express Delivery Van' was available on the car chassis at £175. Yet it is doubtful if even Henry Ford with all his initiative could have imagined a Model T hauling coal, delivering fodder to the cattle boats in Southampton Docks, and operating as a bus. Such was the life of the 1913 vehicle of this chapter.

It was purchased new in 1913 by a carrier in the Southampton area whose name cannot now be traced. But it is known that he disposed of it in part exchange to Ford dealers in St. Mary's Street, Southampton, where it was seen and bought by Austin Dovey of Owlesbury, near Winchester in 1919. Mr Dovey had recently been demobbed from the Army and was building up a carrier's business with the help of a horse-drawn cart. His gratuity paid for the Model T.

Austin Dovey kept the Model T for many years and in 1921 its chassis was extended at the rear by the Baico Chassis Extending Service. This was a specialised operation which required the original rear wheels to be removed and replaced by chain sprockets. Then a new axle with free running wheels was mounted several feet to the rear of the original axle thus providing an extended wheel base to accommodate a longer body. Two substantial roller chains at each side coupled the chain sprockets on the original axle to larger chain sprockets on each rear wheel. This arrangement achieved two modifications: the first being an increased wheel base, and the second an overall gear reduction to enable the standard Model T car chassis to carry at least three times the weight of the original model — albeit with a considerable reduction in top speed.

Obviously, the original small size rear (pneumatic) tyres could not carry such an increase in weight and new rear wheels were fitted; these being supplied with solid tyres, no doubt because of difficulty in obtaining suitable pneumatic tyres at the time. The original front tyres were retained. The lengthened chassis was then fitted with a drop-sided truck body, movable seats to carry 14 persons, and a detachable canopy with celluloid side windows. This adaptable body was built by the forerunners of the Pitt Trailer Company of Barton Stacey, Hampshire.

Many years later when Austin Dovey was in his 80's he talked about this lorry-come-bus with the present owner, and as a consequence of their meeting much of the vehicle's early history is known. Regrettably, Mr Dovey could not remember the name of the first owner although he had known this, but his general recollections of the Ford were very clear. He was able to describe journeys to the Docks at Southampton with hay,straw, mangel-wurzels or turnips for the cattle boats; and he also spoke of his coal-hauling operations in the Whitchurch, Twyford and Southampton districts.

Austin Dovey explained that in the 1920's Owlesbury was a small hamlet boasting no more than six or eight cottages, and his Model T was used for many purposes. He mentioned occasions when it was swept clean of coal dust and transformed into a rural bus with canopy, and detachable slatted wooden seats. In this guise it carried shoppers to the nearest town, or local cricket and football teams to play in away matches.

1913 Model T Ford Rural Bus

The vehicle continued in use until 1933 when its owner was faced with the cost of changing the rear wheels to take pneumatic tyres and with other work necessary after 20 years of use. Indeed, it was the prospect of this expenditure, coupled with route restrictions introduced by new legislation, that forced Mr Dovey to take the old Ford off the road. But not to sell it. He could not bring himself to do this until 1960 when it had been in store for almost 30 years, and even then it was only after much heart-searching that he allowed it to go to a scrap merchant in Hurstbourne Tarrant near Andover.

Fortunately, the vehicle's sojourn at Hurstbourne Tarrant was brief, for it was bought shortly after arrival by Henry Wyatt of Yattendon, Berkshire. Mr Wyatt was a garage proprietor and skilled engineer who, as a young man, had worked in his father's building and haulage company where about 20 Model T vehicles were in use at various times. His experience of the make was considerable, and he was not dismayed by the condition of the 1913 Ford or by the amount of re-building required.

Nevertheless it was 1966 before the restoration was finished. Mr Wyatt was ill for a long time in the early 1960's, and as a result of this set-back and heavy business commitments he was not able to start work on the Model T for several years. But the day came when he could begin, and the entire vehicle was dismantled. All working parts on the engine were stripped down and inspected; the woodwork was repaired where possible and new rear solid tyres were purchased. Mr Wyatt said that a new canopy cover was also necessary as the original was "literally in shreds". Finally, the paintwork was stripped and the bare metal treated with an anti-rust preparation followed by several coats of green enamel — the end result being a marked improvement in the appearance of the old Ford.

Much of the re-building demanded skill, patience and precision; for example Henry Wyatt turned and milled two front chain sprockets out of solid steel. But the work was completed in due time, in fact just in time for the 53-year-old Ford to take part in the Historic Commercial Vehicle Club's annual London to Brighton Run on 1st May, 1966, where it did well. Since that time it has completed every London to Brighton Run and has entered other rallies. It has also been seen at many shows and carnivals, and in three films of which the most notable was 'Our Miss Fred' with Danny La Rue. Mr Wyatt drove the vehicle in a number of shots during the making of all three films. Television viewers may have spotted it in 'The Amazing Mr Blunden' shown on 27th December, 1977.

Yet for all these 'big time' engagements, it is likely that Henry Wyatt's most exciting. outing with the Model T came on 13th August, 1966, when he drove it to a fete in the village of Owlesbury and there met Austin Dovey. Mr Dovey, at 80-odd years of age, was delighted to see his old vehicle and enjoyed riding in it once more. So too did others at the fete; Henry Wyatt met several people who remembered the Ford and were glad to ride in it again despite its solid rear tyres, hard springing and somewhat rugged amenities. One such was Mr Jack White, a farmer of Owlesbury, who had vivid recollections of going to dances in the vehicle in his youth.

Mr Wyatt has described his 1913 Model T as "in good shape for its age", adding that it is capable of an average speed of 20 m.p.h. with maximum at about 27 m.p.h., and petrol consumption of 18 m.p.g. He enjoys driving the vehicle and has tried to trace its early history.

This old vehicle is a good example of the versatile

1913 Model T Ford Rural Bus

Model T Ford which was popular in many countries and in many roles. Its success was most marked in Britain where by 1919 it represented 40% of all vehicles registered.

Specification:
Horsepower	20
Cylinders	4
Bore/stroke	3¾" x 4"

Those readers who are not conversant with the Model T Ford may like to know that there were several unusual features in the construction of the vehicle which seem strange today. It was designed with an unorthodox foot-operated gearbox and fitted with three pedals, two forward gears, reverse gear and a hand-operated throttle lever on the steering column. The left-foot pedal was used for both forward gears, and the centre pedal was the reverse gear. The right-foot pedal operated the foot brake as is customary.

To engage first gear the left-foot pedal (normally the clutch pedal) was pushed in progressively — using firm pressure to hold the gear in for as long as needed. The pedal was released as soon as sufficient speed was reached in first gear, and when right back it engaged top gear via a multi-plate clutch. When this same pedal was half way in, it was at neutral and could be held in this position by pulling the hand brake on.

So, when driving off in a Model T the left-foot pedal would be pushed in progressively, while, at the same time, the hand brake would be released and the hand throttle opened. Once sufficient speed was gained the left pedal was allowed to come back into top gear and the driver could remove his foot and relax — that is until he came to a long steep hill which he had to ascend in low gear with his foot hard down on the left pedal.

In order to use reverse gear the driver would hold neutral with the left-foot pedal, while applying pressure with his right foot on the centre (reverse gear) pedal. The alternating use of these two pedals enabled him to turn his Model T round quickly in little more than its own length without applying the brake. To explain the action more fully: each pedal contracted a band around a drum which housed its respective spur planetary-type gearing, and the slipping of these bands gave a smoother take-off when first applying pressure to the pedals.

This pen-picture of the way to drive a Model T Ford will seem confusing to present-day motorists. Yet past owners of Model Ts always say that they were easy to drive, and that the gear change was quick and quiet at a time when the orthodox gearbox was without syncro-mesh.

The ignition system on the Model T was also different; current was generated by flywheel magneto via four trembler coils, and when the vehicle was running there was sufficient current to light the head lamps. On early models, which were without batteries, oil lamps were used for the side and tail — as is the case with the 1913 bus-come-lorry of this chapter.

These unusual features were all part of the 'personality' of the Model T. But they were not thought to be unusual in 1919 when Austin Dovey bought his, for in that year one in every three vehicles on the road was a Model T.

The Ford Motor Company was mighty proud of its 'Tin Lizzie' and boasted of the model's success — with a singular lack of modesty — in all Company publications. The following extract from the *Ford Times* is a good example:

PLATE 8—1914 Dennis Motor Fire Engine

Owner and Photo: Dennis Motors Limited

PLATE 9—1919 Caledon Lorry

Owner: Nick Baldwin (at wheel)

Photo: The British Petroleum Co. Ltd.

1913 Model T Ford Rural Bus

"We do not sell Ford vehicles solely because they are three times as cheap and more than three times. We sell them because, although they may be at least three times as cheap, they are also at least as good as vehicles three times as dear, in all the qualities of life and speed and comfortable travel that go to make a sound and serviceable road vehicle. At least as good, we said, because modestly we would offer our friendly competitors no affront."

The Model T was in production from October 1908 to May 1927 and more than 15 million were built.

Chapter Three

1914 Dennis Motor Fire Engine
with Turbine-type Pump
A Stalwart Breed

Many different types of road vehicles have been built by Dennis Motors Limited in the last 80 years, but the Company is probably best known for its fire appliances. In fact, its name has been associated with fire-fighting vehicles ever since the 'Dennis Motor Fire Engine with Turbine-type Pump' was introduced in 1908.

In 1908 Dennis Bros., as the Company was then named, had been established for 13 years. It was founded in 1895 when John Dennis and his 17-year-old brother, Herbert Raymond, opened a cycle shop in High Street, Guildford. At that date they had no thought of manufacturing motor vehicles — let alone a fire engine — they were busy producing 'Speed King' and 'Speed Queen' bicycles. But two such enterprising young men could not fail to be excited by the new form of road transport just emerging. They soon began to experiment with motorised tricycles, and evidently met with some success, for in 1898 John Dennis was prosecuted for "driving furiously up Guildford High Street at 16 m.p.h.".

This setback did not dampen the brothers' enthusiasm for motor transport and in 1900 they moved their little Company to larger premises in Guildford and began producing the 'Speed King Motor Quad'. The next logical step was a motor-car, and in 1901 the Dennis car appeared and went on to win the

1914 Dennis Motor Fire Engine

Tilburstow Hill Climb. Other cars followed and the first Dennis commercial vehicle was produced in 1904. This was a 15-cwt box van built on a car chassis for Harrods Ltd. and subsequently exhibited at the Crystal Palace Motor Show. 1904 was also the year of the first Dennis bus and of the Dennis patented worm-driven rear axle.

Progress continued and by 1908 there were Dennis buses, motor-cars and delivery vans. The value of the internal combustion engine for commercial vehicles was generally recognised. Yet there were still fire brigades using horse- or steam-driven appliances, and openings for an efficient motorised fire engine were many when the 'Dennis Motor Fire Engine with Gwynne Turbine-type Pump' was introduced.

The first model was sold to the City of Bradford in 1908. But the sale was not made easily, for the members of the Bradford Fire Brigade Committee did not intend to purchase the City's first motorised fire engine until they were certain of its abilities. They asked for a demonstration, and this was given at the Central Fire Station in Bradford on 18th July, 1908, and reported in the local press:

"Bradford Daily Telegraph", 18th July, 1908.
"At the Central Fire Station at Bradford this morning, some interesting experiments were carried out before the Fire Brigade Committee in connection with the "Dennis" Patent Turbine Fire Engine. It will be remembered that the principle of motor engines has already been adopted by the Committee, and a sum of money has been granted to them for the purchase of a suitable type. The "Dennis" Engine, which came over on "appro." yesterday from the Fireman's Camp at Scarborough, claims to have many advantages. The most interesting part of the machine is the pump, which is of the centrifugal high pressure or turbine type, quite a new departure in fire engines, and is driven by the same engine that drives the chassis. ......The experiments this morning

31

were eminently satisfactory, a powerful jet of water being quickly sent to a height of 100ft. against a very strong breeze. The firemen expressed themselves delighted."

Despite the undoubted success of this demonstation the members of the Bradford Fire Brigade Committee remained uncertain, and another trial was given on the 12th September, 1908. This second demonstration convinced the Committee of the merits of the Dennis engine and, as on the previous occasion, it was well reported in the *Bradford Daily Telegraph:*

"At the request of the Bradford Fire Brigade Committee, Messrs Dennis Bros. of Guildford, who are well known as the pioneers of the Turbine Fire Engine, gave a further demonstration before several members of the Committee yesterday, and very successfully completed every test which was required to conclusively convince the Committee. ...A display of four, three, two and one jets of various size nozzles was successfully performed at the Fire Station, and the flag staff mounted on the top of the 90 feet watch tower was quite easily negotiated, and has, perhaps, never before received such a drenching from underneath.

"The machine was then taken over to Windhill, a distance of three miles, which was completed in the extraordinary short space of five minutes, being driven not recklessly, but with all consideration for other users of the road. On arriving there with its valuable load of Bradford Councillors, numbering eighteen, it immediately proceeded to lift water from a height of 25 feet, and in 1¾ minutes after arrival was delivering two most useful and continuous jets of water....."

This lively report concludes by informing readers that after the demonstration the members of the Bradford Fire Brigade Committee decided unanimously to "stand firm to their recommendation made to the Council recently to purchase a "Dennis" Turbine Fire Engine".

1914 Dennis Motor Fire Engine

The demonstrations at Bradford were the first of many given to local authorities, and Dennis Company records show that before the end of 1908 the new motor fire engine had been demonstrated in the following boroughs:

Hereford
Kingston
Sheffield
Surbiton
Weybridge
Woking

Good reports appeared in the local press after each demonstration — the write-up in the *Woking News and Mail* of the 14th August, 1908, being the most exciting:

"Capt. Sherlock, of the Woking Brigade, arranged for the display by the "Dennis" Turbine Motor Fire Engine. The motor engine was driven across the common and on to the towing path, the suction pipe dropped into the water, the hose run out, and, in about 15 seconds, what appeared to be the bed of the canal was being thrown into the air from two jets. The suction pipe had got into the mud, and the water was as black as ink in consequence. But this incident only served to illustrate one of the many good points of the new machine........"

It is clear that Dennis fire engines performed well during demonstrations, and records prove that they were just as competent in service. For instance, on the 18th June, 1909, the *Bradford Daily Argus* congratulated the City's one-year-old engine on reaching a stack fire at a village 4½ miles from the fire station in under ten minutes. The report went on to explain that the water had to be "driven up a 300 yards' incline" and it added "the turbine faced the work grandly, and sent water out so efficiently that the fire was got under shortly after the Motor had got fairly to work".

The Bradford fire engine was the only one sold by

Rare and Interesting Commercial Vehicles

Dennis Bros. in 1908; but orders were coming in, and in 1909 eight models were built and supplied to the following municipalities: Birmingham
Birkenhead
Christchurch
Fremantle
Glasgow
Kingston (two vehicles)
Rowley Regis, Staffordshire

Thereafter demand grew rapidly, and 49 engines were sold in 1912 — including eight to Sydney, two to the Royal Palace of Siam and three to Brazil.

Production continued during World War 1 and Dennis engines were at work in several war areas. Company archives give the dramatic information that: "Two Dennis Fire Engines were pumping continuously for 10 and 17 days respectively at the great Salonika fire in 1917". And on another page it is noted that 50 Dennis engines were supplied to the London Fire Brigade after the early air raids.

There is no doubt that the Dennis motor turbine fire engine had an important role in the early development of fire-fighting appliances, and the engine featured in this chapter is a good example. It was built in 1914 and sold in that year to Greenall Whitley and Company Limited, brewers of Warrington, Lancashire. It is fitted with a White and Poppe engine, as were all Dennis fire engines of the period; the main water pump is the Gwynne multi-stage turbine type, and there is also a 30 gallon 'first aid' tank from which water is fed to the hose reel by a small gear pump. The Braidwood type body is of Dennis manufacture and can seat eight men: three sitting each side facing outwards with the driver and chief officer seated in front.

Greenall Whitley and Company bought this 1914 Dennis fire engine when it was new for £845. The

Dennis terms of business were one-third of the price on order with the balance due on delivery, and the retail price included the service of an instructor for one week free-of-charge provided his "board and lodgings" were paid by the purchaser of the vehicle. In addition, there was a special guarantee of 10 years on the Worm Gear if "not subjected to misuse".

The Greenall Whitley Company had the advice of an instructor for a week and also, like all owners of Dennis motor fire engines, received a remarkably detailed manual. This provided all the usual technical data, plus a long list of "do's and don'ts" covering several pages. The driver was exhorted to take a "studied interest" in the running of the vehicle under his control and to deal at once with any detail requiring attention, thereby avoiding the "evils of neglected repair".

Such evils were avoided at Greenall Whitley Limited, because the 1914 vehicle played a major part in the firm's fire-fighting operations for many years and was not disposed of until 1951. In 1975 the Managing Director of the Company, Mr J. D. Pritchard-Barrett, explained that it was manned by employees who lived in cottages close to the brewery in Wilderspool Causeway, Warrington, and that these cottages are still known as "the firemen's houses". Company records show that the vehicle also did useful work putting out farm fires, usually haystacks, in the country district around Warrington.

It was July 1951 when the old engine changed hands, the new owners being the Old Trafford Motor Engineering Co. Ltd. of Manchester — north western area distributors for Dennis vehicles. Mr D. A. T. Hughes, Managing Director of the Company, told me that he and his colleagues were happy to have the aged vehicle and entered it in rallies and fetes. But there were times when it broke down due to "fuel supply problems occasioned by long periods of disuse'', and Mr. Hughes said that it was difficult to keep the vehicle looking clean and polished because, as he pointed out, the considerable area of brass-work "persistently succumbed to Manchester weather".

So when Mr John Sutton, then Works Director at Dennis Motors, suggested that the old fire engine should be handed to the Dennis apprentices to strip and rebuild, Mr Hughes agreed that this would be the best course. Arrangements were then made, and the vehicle was taken from Manchester to Guildford by transporter in 1960.

I met Mr John C. R. Dennis (grandson of one of the founders of the Dennis Company) at the works in Guildford during October 1975, and he described how the apprentices, working under supervision, stripped the vehicle down to the "last proverbial nut and bolt" and then rebuilt it. He explained that this was a part-time job for three years, the end result being a perfectly restored 1914 fire engine that was still original with the exception of some sections of timber framing, upholstery, and the solid tyres which had to be renewed.

This interesting commercial vehicle has been used and seen many times since it was restored: it has taken part in rallies and shows; in exhibitions, fund-raising events and several London to Brighton Runs. It was a prominent exhibit in the 1975 Interfire Exhibition held at Olympia, and John Dennis mentioned that it was the only fire appliance in the Veteran and Vintage Drive into Europe organised in support of the "Fanfare into Europe" celebrations in 1973.

The vehicle is now 64 years of age and has the classic appearance of a picture-book fire engine; solid and reliable with gleaming red paint and brass-work. In its day it would have given a sense of security to all

1914 Dennis Motor Fire Engine

those who watched as it hurried through the streets with bell ringing. It is not the oldest Dennis fire engine existing in good condition today, and John Dennis believes that there may be eight such vehicles in different countries.

Dennis fire engines of the early 1900's are appropriate reminders of a period of great development in the history of fire-fighting expertise. It is good that one or two can still be seen in running order.

Specification details are:

Engine.	6.6 litre, 'T' head, side valve, inlet and exhaust on opposite sides.
Cylinders.	Four.
Bore.	127 mm.
Stroke.	130mm.
Ignition.	Bosch H.T. magneto. Trembler coil for starting.
Carburettor.	Claudel Hobson updraught.
Gearbox.	4-speed crash type.
Brakes.	Rear wheels only (foot brake on transmission drum behind gearbox and hand brake operating on rear wheel drums).
Wheels.	Wooden.
Tyres.	Solid rubber.
Maximum safe speed	30 m.p.h.
Fuel	Petrol.
Fuel tank capacity	18 gallons.
Weight.	3½ tons.
Locker capacity.	750 ft. of 2¾ ins. hose and other equipment.

Chapter Four

1919 Caledon Lorry
A Veteran of Many Roles

This Caledon lorry has the distinction of being a rare—
possibly unique—commercial vehicle. It also has a
strange history that ranges through use as a lorry, a
charabanc, an ice-cream emporium, a lake-side holiday
chalet and, finally, a dilapidated shack-like home for
an old man. Today, it is restored to its original
appearance.

The history of the firm that built Caledon lorries is
itself somewhat diverse. Scottish Commercial Cars
began as motor dealers in Glasgow, and launched into
the production of lorries when commercial vehicles
were in short supply during World War 1. To this end
the firm set up Caledon Motors Limited and, having
acquired a disused roller-skating rink in Duke Street,
Glasgow, began to build Caledon lorries. Production
was never large; but the Company attracted a few
notable customers such as the United States Expedit-
ionary Forces, the Russian Government and S.J.
Morland & Sons the match manufacturers, who each
took a few vehicles. The firm's best customer, however, was the British Petroleum Company and Caledon
lorries were seen delivering BP petrol to garages in
two-gallon cans at a time when petrol pumps were just
emerging.

Caledon Motors made reasonable progress in the
early years and by 1919 some 400 people were
employed. Yet sales were never more than moderate,

and the firm was hit badly when Government agencies released large numbers of surplus commercial vehicles onto the second-hand market at low prices at the end of the War. The Company was too under-capitalised to withstand this competition in a period of post-war depression and was obliged to close down briefly in 1922. It managed to struggle back into operation before the end of that year—albeit under the name of Scottish Commercial Cars and with a staff of no more than 40.

Thereafter the pitfalls were many, and the firm could only stagger on despite the ready support of a responsible workforce. This is apparant in an article in *Old Motor [Vol 9 No 3]* by Alex McKee who worked on Caledons for a time. When writing about the Company's situation in 1923 he says that there were "no more than 25 to 30 of us all told", and adds:

> "It was a case of everybody doing whatever was required to be done.

> "They (the management) drove the few of us hard, but themselves just as hard. Hours did not matter and we all wanted to see the old firm weather the storm."

Sadly these efforts were ineffectual and the Company continued to slip downhill. Mr. McKee writes that in the winter of 1926/27 the future looked "very bleak", and he relates the following incident which highlights the firm's desperate situation:

> ". . . . . I remember one pay-day seeing a fitter clutching a new magneto under his overalls in case he had to 'take it in lieu of pay'."

Scottish Commercial Cars/Caledon Motors was run by its two principal directors: Harry and Edmund

Tanish, and Mr McKee points out that as far as he could see there was "never any extravagance in the firm"—just "hard work." Yet the end was inevitable, and in 1927 what remained of the business was bought by the Garrett Company of Leiston, Suffolk.

Richard Garrett & Sons was well known for the manufacture of steam waggons and it is probable that the directors were becoming aware of the advantages of the internal combustion engine, hence their interest in the sinking Caledon works. Whatever the motivation, the venture was not successful; although at least two Caledon/Garrett petrol vehicles were built before the project was written off as a failure and the production of Caledon commercial vehicles came to an end.

Fortunately the Caledon lorry of this chapter was built some years before these dismal days. It is now owned by Nick Baldwin who acquired it in 1970. Mr Baldwin is an authority on historic commercial vehicles and has made great efforts to trace the history of his Caledon. His researches have shown that it was delivered when new to the Lion Garage, Bridge Street, Warrington, Lancashire, before being sold to Messrs W. & A. Ashton and registered as a goods vehicle. Ashton's were building contractors with premises at Wilderspool, The Causeway, Warrington, and were in existence from 1908 to 1952.

It has not been possible to establish the length of time that the lorry was owned by Ashton's, although from subsequent information Nick believes that it may have been hired to British Petroleum for a while. Certainly, it could not have been used to any great extent because there was little evidence of wear when the vehicle was restored.

Taxation authorities in the Warrington district were able to tell Mr Baldwin that the lorry was recorded as a charabanc in 1926, but they could not provide the name of the owner at this period. However, the vehicle's existence as a charabanc must have been short-lived because the present owner's enquiries brought him into contact with some showmen in the Lake District who remembered the Caledon in use as an "ice cream emporium" in 1927/28.

At this time the vehicle was not licensed for road use. Its lorry and, presumably, its charabanc body had disappeared, and it wore an ornate ice-cream parlour outfit that had been made by an Italian living in the Lake District. Nick Baldwin explained that this, seemingly, drastic alteration may not have been as fundamental as it sounds. The transformation could have been accomplished by roofing the charabanc body, painting it lavishly in cream and gold, and embellishing with carved end-pieces and cornice. But, however the change was achieved, the end result must have been gaudy and eye-catching since the showmen were able to describe the vehicle's appearance with vivid detail despite the passing of many years.

This chameleon-like lorry was obviously a success as an ice-cream parlour, but the length of its service in this role remains unknown. It is next heard of in the 1930's when it had assumed the guise of a lake-side holiday chalet. In this capacity the Caledon had a corrugated iron and felt roof and was hedged around with a flower border and verandah. Mr Baldwin has been told that it made a reasonably attractive week-end bungalow; but deteriorated in later years when it became the home of a solitary old man who lived in it in increasing squalor. Much of the vehicle's bodywork had rotted away before this period of its existence came to an end.

The elderly occupant had long since gone when the

present owner heard of the vehicle in 1970. He was telephoned by a friend who had talked with two scrap metal merchants in a public house while they tried to sell the wheels of the derelict old lorry — for garden ornaments!

When Nick Baldwin was given a description of the vehicle and learned that it was about to be demolished he immediately "jumped into the car" and began what proved to be a 10-hour journey; a journey that ended with a shock when he saw the Caledon's dilapidated appearance. All partitions behind the bulkhead had been demolished. The seat, petrol tank and steering column had gone — Nick pointed out that past residents of the lorry had, at least, been spared the annoyance of a steering column protruding into their living-room. Hand brake and gear lever were also missing, and pieces of these with part of the steering column were found in the undergrowth, which was remarkable since they may have been thrown there in the 1930's.

The rotten wood, roofing and verandah had been burned and the vehicle was about to be taken away for demolition when Mr Baldwin arrived. He had to make an offer at once. This was accepted with the proviso that the lorry was removed without delay — which proved difficult until a local coal merchant was persuaded to transport it on the back of his coal lorry to an old railway marshalling yard. It was some weeks later when the Caledon arrived at the new owner's home in Oxfordshire.

When he examined the lorry and stripped the engine Nick saw that it had been little used, indeed there were several factors that indicated that it had not been used on the road since 1926. The engine, for example, showed few signs of wear, it did not require reboring and the crankshaft was in good

condition. In addition the lorry was still fitted with
acetylene lamps, and it is likely that it would have been
converted to electric if it had been used much after
1926; likewise the wheels had not been converted to
take pneumatic tyres. The name Caledon was still
distinct on all foot pedals and there was no evidence
that the vehicle had been registered for road use
later than 1926.

So Mr Baldwin had good reason to be pleased with
his rare old lorry; but it was some years before he could
begin the restoration and he spent this period "hunting
around" for missing accessories such as the horn,
side and tail lamps. There was also the problem of
knowing exactly how the vehicle should look, and he
was fortunate when his advertisement in *Old Motor*
resulted in a call from Mr Bob Whitehead.

Mr Whitehead is the author of *Garretts of Leiston*
and so had studied the Caledon records while writing
about the purchase of the ailing firm. From his
research material he was able to produce a list of
every customer who bought a Caledon lorry, and as
British Petroleum had purchased the greatest number
Nick wrote to the Company asking if there were any
photographs and/or specifications of Caledons in
the archives. The response was swift. Within a few
days a representative of BP arrived at Mr Baldwin's
home and together they were able to find a counterpart
of the 1919 lorry.

Restoration could then begin. Mr John Smith of
Banbury College of Art produced exact drawings for
the re-building of body and cab and he assisted Nick
Baldwin with the work. The major part of the restoration consisted of replacing woodwork from chassis-
level up and, with the help of Mr Michael North from
a local garage, the three men completed the restoration
just in time for the Historic Commercial Vehicle Club's

1975 London to Brighton Run. 'Just in time' is accurate, for the engine was not tried until two days before the Run. In all probability the engine had not been in use for 50 years and there was anxiety about its performance — followed by much relief when it back-fired after six nervous pulls on the starting handle. Adjustments were soon made to the timing, the engine was running and the lorry went forth for a brief trial run of about one mile.

Then followed a hectic day on the usual vast number of last minute jobs, and the lorry was taken to London in good order for the Brighton Run on the next morning. Because the Caledon is slow it was one of the first to be sent off by the Stewards just after 7.00 a.m. It still carried its original registration number — ED 1709 — which had been allocated by the Warrington authorities in 1919 and was still on solid rubber tyres, thereby restricting the driver to a legal speed limit of 12 m.p.h. Mr Baldwin says the vehicle is capable of travelling slightly faster in favourable conditions.

All seemed 'set fair' for a steady drive to Brighton, but the journey proved otherwise and Nick has des-cribed it as "slightly nightmarish". This state of affairs was due to the number of times that the magneto became "gummed up" through the heat of the engine softening the insulating coating of the armature. Mr Baldwin and his co-driver were obliged to clean the magneto at the roadside at five-mile intervals, and it was 3.30 p.m. when the lorry reached the finishing post — just after the judging closed. It had taken a long eight hours to cover 50 miles and the prospect of the return journey was not attractive. The Caledon was taken home by transporter.

Since that day the old lorry has been improved progressively and, in its owner's words, is now "a nice thing to drive''. It has taken part in rallies and shows — and been much admired.

At the time of writing the vehicle is painted in BP livery (predominantly green with red wheels, bonnet and scuttle) and carries a load of 450 two-gallon petrol cans of 1919 era — these having been found by British Petroleum in a chemical works at Stoke-on-Trent. When in use in 1920 Caledon lorries of this type carried 500 x two-gallon cans of petrol.

The vehicle has recently been photographed outside the old roller-skating rink in Duke Street, Glasgow, where it was built. I am told that this erstwhile factory is now a homely hostel, regardless of its somewhat grandiose name 'Great Easton Hotel'; but no matter since it, like the old Caledon lorry, manages to keep going — in one guise or another.

It is good that this 59-year-old commercial vehicle has been restored and once more assumes the respectable appearance of a lorry. It is equally good that it will be active and — most important — will be seen, because it is thought to be the only restored Caledon lorry in existence. No more than 700/750 were built, so the prospect of other survivors must be remote.

Specification details are:

Cylinders.	Four.
Engine.	6.4-litre.
Bore /Stroke.	120 mm x 140 mm.
Load Capacity.	Four tons.
Braking system.	Foot brake pedal operates copper-lined shoes on drum at rear of gearbox. Hand brake leaver operates shoes on rear drums.

Ràre and Interesting Commercial Vehicles

Tyres.	Solid.
Speed.	12 m.p.h. (legal).
Fuel.	Petrol (the cheapest grade suffices).
Fuel consumption.	5 m.p.g.

Chapter Five

1920 Lacre L-type Sweeper
Sweeping to Success

It hardly seems apt to describe a road-sweeper as 'rare and exciting' but both adjectives fit this 1920 Lacre L-type sweeper. The L-type was an exciting development in road sweeping when it was introduced in 1919, and the 1920 model of this chapter is believed to be the oldest sweeper of its type in existence in working order.

The Lacre Company was well established by 1919, having been founded in 1902 in the Long Acre district of London by Claude Browne, the son of a wealthy printer. Claude Browne was young; he was fascinated by the rapidly developing motor-car and he intended to make his career in this new industry. He named his firm the Long Acre Car Company, but this was soon changed to the Lacre Motor Car Co., and the firm's address to Poland Street, Soho where the L'Acre car was built. However, production of this model was brief, for Claude Brown recognised the motor vehicle's potential for commercial use, and in 1904 he produced the first Lacre van.

Few people shared Claude Browne's enthusiasm for motorised commercial vehicles, and his vans and lorries did not find ready markets at first. Many tradesmen of the period were satisfied with their horse-drawn service and were slow to see the advantages of petrol-driven transport. It took time and money, plus all Claude

Browne's enterprise to persuade a number of big departmental stores to abandon their horse-drawn delivery vehicles, and his first success came with the sale of a lorry to Shoolbred & Co., a leading store of the day. But the sale was not made easily, in fact it was not made until Shoolbred's had enjoyed the use of a Lacre lorry for a free trial period of six weeks, and one of the Company's roundsmen had been taught to drive a motor vehicle by Lacre mechanics. This last activity became an essential element in many sales in the early 1900's and the Lacre Company taught numbers of horse-drivers to handle the new petrol-driven road vehicles.

After this breakthrough sales began to mount, and the Lacre Motor Car Co. was able to make much of the fact that its vehicles were manufactured specifically for commercial use — that they were not 'converted motor-cars'. This point being emphasised in the Company's early brochure:

> "It must be clear to everyone that the construction of a good Commercial Vehicle should differ from that of a Pleasure Chassis in many ways. The conditions of use, weights carried, continual wear and different strains to a Motor Van soon shake to pieces a chassis constructed on pleasure lines."

Many people were prejudiced against motor vehicles in the early 1900's, and others did not understand the functions of this new form of transport. So publicity was vital, and motor manufacturers had faith in the efficacy of demonstration runs. The Lacre Motor Car Co. was no exception, and in 1905 a 15-cwt van loaded with goods to a weight of 17 cwt, plus the driver and a passenger, made a non-stop run from London to Swansea — a journey of 214 miles that was accomplished in 18 hours. In the same year a 16-cwt delivery

van toured major towns and cities giving demon-
stations of the vehicle's capabilities to tradespeople
and attracting as much attention as possible.

Eventually hard work, publicity and a well-built
product brought results, and it is evident from the 1907
catalogue that orders were flowing in:

> "We would mention that, up to the time of going to press,
> we have been favoured with orders from Messrs Shoolbred
> for as many as thirty of our vans; Harrods Ltd. have placed
> orders for twenty-six "Lacre" vehicles; Messrs Carter,
> Paterson & Co. have already eleven of our vans on the
> road . . . . . ."

Progress continued and by 1909 the Lacre Company
was throughly established. Its list of customers was
growing and included Schweppes Ltd., and the Siamese
Government. Its range of vehicles was also growing,
and it became necessary to look for larger premises
out of London. These proved difficult, and it was
decided to buy land at Letchworth in Hertfordshire
and build a factory. When the Company moved into
this building in 1910 it was thought to be the first
factory in Britain to be designed specially for the
manufacture of commercial vehicles.

Once installed at Letchworth the firm began to
extend its range of vehicles even further, and by the
beginning of 1914 there were 19 different models in
production covering a variety of uses, as the Company's
catalogue of the period declared in glowing phrases:

> "Thousands of miles of roads are annually swept by "Lacre"
> Sweeping Machines, sprayed by "Lacre" Water Carts,
> and thousands of tons of refuse are removed by "Lacre"
> Tipping Wagons. Many gullies are cleaned by "Lacre"
> Vacuum Gully Emptying Equipments. Overhead electric

49

4

cables are repaired by the use of "Lacre" Tower Wagons. Telegraph Poles are erected by "Lacre" Pole Erecting Outfits and "Lacre" Rescue Wagons are employed on Mines rescue work."

The first World War brought more work and the Company's Chief Engineer, J. S. Drewery, was subsequently decorated by the Belgium Government for his designs of special pontoon equipment for the Belgium army. Mr Drewery had been a pioneer in the motor industry having worked for a firm handling De Dion-Bouton cars in 1899 when he was 17. He joined Lacre's in 1911 and remained with the firm until 1922; his most important work in this period was the design of the L-type 3-wheeled sweeper — the vehicle that was to have such an important role in the future of the Company.

4-wheeled road sweepers had been built for some years before the 3-wheeled L-type (single wheel at rear) was introduced in 1919. It was a new development in sweeping machines, having a wide area of sweep, small turning circle and exceptional manoeuverability. The driver's seat was situated at the rear of the chassis with the controls fitted around the steering-wheel, thus enabling him to control the direction of the sweep and avoid overlapping or unswept areas. In addition, the brush could be replaced by a scraper, squeegee or snowplough.

A water tank of about 100 gallons capacity was built into the centre of the chassis giving the vehicle a somewhat square appearance. Water was piped from the tank to a gear-driven pump attached to the rear end of the gearbox, and from there through two spraying nozzles attached to the front of the vehicle at a pressure of about 20 lbs per square inch.

Mr Donald A. Thomas, who has been Managing Director of the Lacre Company since 1948, told me that the L-type sweeper was in its day "a new breakthrough as far as sweeping was concerned", and he added that it was this machine, more than any other, that "brought the Company into the municipal field". The L-type undoubtedly helped the firm to survive the depression of the 1920's and it was in production—with modifications such as pneumatic tyres—until 1947.

The first L-type 3-wheeled sweeper to be built was sold to the Municipality of Bergen in Norway for £300 and was delivered for shipping on 31st August, 1920. By the end of that year 40 L-types had been completed and sold, including the sweeper of this chapter which was bought by the Burgh of Motherwell and Wishaw in Scotland. This hardy vehicle remained with the Burgh for 32 years and was in service for almost the entire period. During these years it became well-known in the Motherwell and Wishaw district, and it was a matter of pride to the Cleansing Department to keep it in good running order. But in 1952 the Council decided that it had to go, and the 32-year-old sweeper was sold to a local greyhound stadium where it was used to sweep the track.

In 1953 Donald Thomas was startled to hear that an old Lacre sweeper — once part of the Motherwell and Wishaw Council fleet — was working in a greyhound stadium and he decided to investigate. An enquiry to the Council produced the chassis and engine numbers; and Mr T. Johnstone, Director of the Council's Cleansing Department, examined the vehicle and confirmed that it was in reasonable condition. These details were sufficient for Mr Thomas. He made an offer to the stadium without seeing the sweeper and after negotiation bought it for £40.

So the old sweeper returned to its manufacturer having been at work for 33 years and, at an average sweeping speed of 3 to 4 miles per hour, having swept about

Rare and Interesting Commercial Vehicles
200,000 miles of road.

When the vehicle was examined at Lacre's it was found that one or two minor parts were missing, but no major restoration was needed, and the sweeper was then painted in the colours of the Lacre demonstrators of the 1920's, i.e. two shades of blue with gold lettering.

Since 1953 the old L-type sweeper has been on show in several exhibitions including the Public Works and Municipal Services Exhibition at Olympia in 1956. Other highlights include the 1971 Historic Commercial Vehicle Club's London to Brighton Run when it completed the route in 6½ hours, and an exhibition of old and new sweepers staged by the Herefordshire County Council in 1973. The vehicle was completely reconditioned in 1974 and has subsequently taken part in several London to Brighton Runs. Donald Thomas believes it to be "the oldest sweeper known to exist in working order" and he hopes that it will be seen in exhibitions and runs for many years to come.

The Lacre Company has been established at St. Albans, Hertfordshire since 1959 and the aged L-type is displayed in the show-room. Its sedate appearance, with sentry box type cab and solid tyres. is very different from the present range of Lacre cleansing vehicles, but it is not likely that the Company will ever again produce a model that will be in production for over a quarter of a century.

A total of 422 L-type sweepers was sold from 1920 to 1947. The first was purchased by the Norwegian city of Bergen for £300 in August 1920, and the last by the County Borough of Manchester for £1,460 in December 1947. A remarkable record.

Specification details are:

PLATE 10—1920 Lacre L-type Sweeper

Photo: Theodore Greville Studios

Owner: Lacre Limited

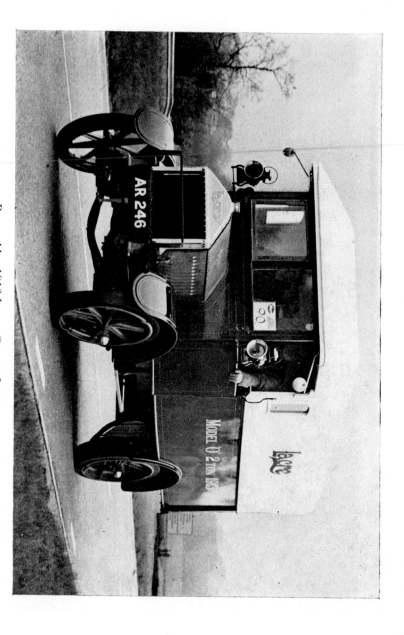

Owner: Lacre Limited

PLATE 11—1913 Lacre O-type Lorry

Photo: Tim Farebrother

Cylinders	Four.
Bore	69 m.m.
Stroke	120 m.m.
Wheels	Three (steelspoked).
Tyres:	Solid Rubber.
Front	100 x 720.
Rear	90 x 720 (one wheel twin-tyred).
Fuel	Petrol.
Type of Body	Sentry box type cab for one person.
Unladen weight	1 ton 12 cwt.
Overall length	12 ft. 4 ins.
Overall width without brush	6 ft. 2 ins.
Diameter of brush	23 ins.
Width of sweep	6 ft.
Capacity of water tank	100 galls approx.

Visitors to the Lacre Company will see that this **1920** sweeper is in good company. It stands next to a **1913** Lacre O-type 2-ton lorry whose history began when it was one of a number of O-type lorries commandeered by the War Office for use in World War 1. After the Armistice the vehicle was acquired by William Whiteley Ltd., London provision merchants, who used it until gearbox damage in the middle 1930's put an end to the vehicle's active life. Thereafter it spent 30 years in a farmyard as a store for pig food and was in poor condition when it came back to the Lacre Company in 1967.

Restoration of the 1913 lorry began at once and was carried out by Mr Albert Abbott who was Works Manager of the Lacre Company until his retirement in 1963. Mr Abbott spent one day a week at the factory working on the lorry, and made components in his own home workshop.

Today this aged solid-tyred lorry is in splendid condition and has taken part in many rallies and exhibitions, often in company with the 1920 L-type sweeper. It has been driven in London to Brighton Runs and has done well, maintaining an average speed of 12 m.p.h., with an occasional 'spurt' at 15 m.p.h.

The O-type lorry was probably the best-known general commercial vehicle produced by Lacre Ltd. Many hundreds of the model were built before, during and after the First World War and were used for a variety of purposes. It seems appropriate, therefore, that this vehicle has been driven in London to Brighton Runs by Mr. Donald Thomas who joined the Lacre Company in 1947 and has been at its head ever since he was appointed Managing Director in 1948.

Chapter Six

1924 Morris One-Ton Lorry
The First of Many

By the early 1920's Morris cars and vans were seen everywhere in Britain, and the renowned 'bullnose' Cowley had outsold all its competitors. Yet the Morris Company had never built a heavy commercial vehicle; in fact, a vehicle in the 1 to 2½ ton range had never been manufactured in the United Kingdon, and overseas makes such as Ford, Renault and Chevrolet had a secure hold on the British market.

This state of affairs was a challenge to William Morris who decided to build a one-ton commercial chassis. With this objective he founded Morris Commercial Cars Limited and installed his company in Foundry Lane, Birmingham, having taken over the factory of E. G. Wrigley & Co., component manufacturers, for the purpose. Once established, the new company was quick to launch a prototype one-ton lorry for demonstration.

News of the first Morris lorry made headlines in the motor trade press, and on the 28th January, 1924, '*Motor Transport*' published an article entitled:

A Morris One-Tonner
First illustrated description of a new one-ton chassis introduced by British maker with large private car output.

Rare and Interesting Commercial Vehicles

This write-up appeared after an exhaustive road test which obviously impressed the journalist since he described the new commercial vehicle as of "no small importance", and went on to point out that the Morris Company intended "to place this industrial machine upon as high a plane as their touring cars in the matter of quality, price and performance". The power unit (engine, clutch and gearbox) was substantially the same as that on the Morris-Oxford car and *'Motor Transport'* mentioned the advantages of this measure. It explained that the Morris engine had a well-earned reputation for sturdiness and reliability, and that its use in the commercial chassis ensured that owners would have "all the benefits of high-grade quantity production".

Other road tests and write-ups followed quickly, all agreeing that the first Morris one-ton chassis was a valuable addition to the British commercial motor industry. What is more, the model lived up to this reputation in production. It sold at about £255 and became very popular in this country and overseas. In the late 1920's and early 1930's more than 100 one-ton lorries were built each week and the model continued in production, with some alterations, until the Second World War.

Thousands of Morris one-ton commercial vehicles were built, but none was as important as the first. This prototype — with its distinctive chassis number 001 — was tested and exhibited all over Britain during the first 12 months of its life and is still in working order.

Today, this notable Morris lorry belongs to Pat Kennett, editor of *'Truck'* magazine, who has traced its history. He described its first, and very successful, year as a demonstrator, and spoke of the years that followed when the vehicle was part of the Morris Com-

1924 Morris One-Ton Lorry

pany's commercial fleet and carried engines from the Morris engine factory in Coventry to the assembly plant at Cowley, Oxford. There are people who still remember seeing the lorry piled high with engines, and Mr Kennett was told that it carried 18 engines on each trip, all crated and stacked lengthways in three two-storey rows, making a total load of over two tons. This load was carried regularly for over ten years and for about 250,000 miles; surely a remarkable feat for a one-ton chassis. Furthermore the vehicle still has its original engine which has been reconditioned.

001 was taken off the road in 1939, but not out of service, and its next ten years were spent carrying parts and castings round the Morris factory at Adderley Park, Birmingham. It was 1949 when the Company at last decided that the vehicle's working life was over, and it was then parked in the corner of a shed at Adderley Park and forgotten for some 15 years.

The historic value of this first Morris lorry was not recognised until the mid 1960's when there was an upsurge of interest in aged vehicles, and by that period it was in a sorry state. 25 years of work, followed by 15 years in the corner of a dusty shed, had left their mark and much rebuilding was necessary. This was carried out by Morris Company apprentices working under supervision, and as soon as the rebuilding was finished the old lorry became an attraction at carnivals and exhibitions. It also had the distinction of being tested for a second time by *'Motor Transport'*, and on this occasion was the subject of a light-hearted road test which was featured in the Christmas issue of the magazine.

It cannot be said that the old vehicle aroused as much interest during the 1960's as it had in 1924 when it was the first one-ton truck to be built in Britain; but it nevertheless had a useful, albeit small, role in projecting the image of Morris vehicles. Yet even this modest acclaim was short-lived, and the lorry gradually dropped out of notice. Why this happened is not clear, but it seems likely that the people responsible for looking after it left the Company. In any event, the old commercial vehicle was once more left to rot in the corner of a shed, and it remained there until the Morris Company decided to close its Adderley Park factory.

Clearing out on a massive scale following this decision, with the result that vast heaps of scrap and obsolete vehicles, including the once famous number one, were shifted out into the yard to await the scrap dealers. It then seemed that 001 must end up in a breaker's yard, and this would have been its fate if Pat Kennett had not seen it while working on a magazine assignment at the British Railways depot next door to the Morris factory.

Mr Kennett had been a British Leyland apprentice, and in 1950/1 he was taken with other apprentices on an educational trip to the Morris Commercial Works in Birmingham. While there he noticed: "a tatty old motor in a corner", and being interested in aged vehicles he made enquiries and learned that it was the prototype Morris one-ton lorry. Since that time he has had glimpses of the vehicle, and he recognised it immediately when he saw it half buried under heaps of scrap in 1971.

It was obvious to Pat Kennett that swift action was necessary if the lorry was to be saved from the breaker's yard, and he made an offer to the Morris Company. This was accepted without difficulty and 001 had its first change of owner.

The vehicle was now 47 years of age and again in poor condition. Since restoration in the mid 1960's it had been neglected, roughly treated and finally damaged when shifted out to the yard with other old vehicles and scrap material. Mr Kennett found that the back of the cab was pushed in, the wings were crumpled, the bonnet was right down on top of the engine and the cooling tubes on the front of the radiator were cracked. In addition, the engine had been run when the oil pump was broken, with the result that bearings needed re-metalling.

Altogether there was a good deal of rebuilding to be done, and the new owner did most of it himself with the exception of specialised jobs such as making new timing gears. Some 2,000 hours of work were needed and, as this was a spare time job, it was 1974 before the restoration was complete. However, the final result is impressive and well worth all Mr Kennett's efforts.

The old vehicle now looks pleasant and well-preserved; yet still retains its original appearance of a strong, practical working lorry — which is what it is. And there is evidence of its industrial background in the many old pieces of scrap and swarf embedded in the hard wood of the body. These have been dressed over and are permanent reminders of Adderley Park days.

Pat Kennett enjoyed restoring his old lorry and he has no doubt that the long hours of work and effort were worthwhile. He told me that there is a great deal to be learned from restoring engineering of any sort, and explained that much can be gained by understanding the original thought that creates a mechanical contrivance. He added, "with new metallurgy applied to old ideas it is sometimes possible to find solutions to today's engineering problems".

This is a professional view of the advantages of restoration, and is comparable with the layman's pleasure at the sight of any well-preserved machine that can still perform the task for which it was built. Certainly, old 001 has been seen and admired many times since Mr

Kennett finished the rebuilding. It has taken part in every London to Brighton Run, in a couple of Manchester to Harrogate Runs and in a vast number of rallies in this country and Europe.

At the time of writing 001 is in the Science Museum in London, where it is a prime exhibit in a special display commemorating the centenary of the birth of William Morris. When this is over the vehicle will become part of the Donington collection.

The first Morris one-ton lorry was important in the history of British commercial motor transport and it is good that it is still in existence.

Specification details are:

Cylinders	Four
Bore	75 mm.
Stroke	102 mm.
Ignition	Magneto.
Gearbox	3-speed.
Final drive	Overhead worm.
Brakes	Foot and Hand. Expanding in rear wheel drums.
Tyres	Pneumatic.
Chassis weight	About 18 cwt.
Speed (today)	27 m.p.h. (flat out).
Fuel (today)	22 m.p.g.

PLATE 12—1924 Morris One-Ton Lorry

Owner: Pat Kennett (at time of writing) *Photo*: Elsam, Mann & Cooper (Manchester) Limited

PLATE 13—1925 Dennis 4-Ton Open-Top Double-Deck Bus

Owner: Prince Marshall

Photo: The Press Association Limited

Chapter Seven

1925 Dennis 4-Ton Open-Top Double-Deck Bus
A much-travelled 'Independent'

Any history of the London Independent Bus Companies
must make confused reading, for they sold out, were
bought up, or merged with one another at an alarming
rate; and the biography of 1925 Dennis bus, XX 9591,
is just as involved.

The early history of this attractive open-top double-
deck bus is in two sections because the chassis and
body began life on separate vehicles. The chassis was
licensed XX9591 on 9th April, 1925, and belonged to
a Mr. W. H. Cook who traded as the Dominion
Omnibus Company until he sold his licence and his
Dennis bus to the London General Omnibus Company
on 20th May, 1926. At that time 'London General'
used A.E.C. (Associated Equipment Company)
vehicles and the year-old Dennis bus was passed to
Redburns Motor Services of Enfield, Middlesex,
where it remained until it was sold to the London
Public Omnibus Company on 21st June, 1928.

Meanwhile the body, which had been built by
Christopher Dodson of Willesden, was part of an
identical Dennis 48-seater bus — registration XW 8201.
This vehicle was owned by E. Flower & Son Ltd., of
Kilburn who operated under the name of Paragon, and
the Paragon Company was bought up by the London
Public Omnibus Company late in 1927 together with
Dennis bus XW 8201.

So by the end of June 1928 both XX 9591 and XW 8201 were in the London Public Omnibus Company's fleet, and this was the situation on the 11th December, 1929, when 'London Public' was absorbed by the mighty London General Omnibus Service. The next change came in July 1930 when these two identical Dennis buses were sent with others to the L.G.O.C. workshops at Chiswick for a major overhaul and the body of XW 8201 was fitted to chassis XX 9591.

When XX 9591 emerged after the body change it was newly painted in the red livery of the London General Omnibus Company, and was back on Route 529 which had been its route with 'London Public'. It remained on this service until the beginning of 1932, when it was transferred to Route 96 for a few months before being sold for scrap in July of that year.

Seven years seem a short time for the working life of a bus. But the 1920's were years of great technical development in the motor-bus industry, and there are many examples of progress made in this period; examples such as tne two given below which have been taken from the archives of Dennis Motors Limited and refer to vehicles manufactured by that Company:

"1925 — First pneumatic-tyred bus passed by the authorities in London.

"1926 — First bus with brakes on all four wheels passed for London service."

The rate of development was such that a bus could easily become obsolete in seven years, and it was taken for granted that XX 9591 had come to the end of its active life when it was sold in July 1932 to a smallholder in Wickford, Essex, and parked on his land. Nothing was heard of this vehicle in the decades

1925 Dennis 4-Ton Open-Top Double Deck Bus

that followed and it is not known if it was ever driven again; what is certain is that it had been used as a garden shed for a long time when it was seen in derelict condition near Wickford during 1970 by Mr Prince Marshall, the publisher of *Old Motor* magazine.

The finding of this aged bus is a strange little story in itself. It came about in the spring of 1970 when two young children living near to Wickford were exploring the overgrown garden of the house next door to them. Both the house and the garden had been neglected since the owner died some years earlier, and the garden, with its ramshackle buildings and overgrown paths, was an exciting playgound for the children. It was especially thrilling when they came across a derelict vehicle hemmed-in on either side by broken-down sheds and hidden beneath a mass of brambles and grass, and they rushed home to tell their parents that they had found "a tram". Needless to say, their parents doubted this until they saw the old bus for themselves;but once convinced they lost no time in seeking advice, and Prince Marshall was soon on the site.

Mr Marshall has been concerned in the preservation of old London buses since the middle 1950's and has acquired several specimens. Therefore, he was a good person to approach about the Dennis vehicle, and he was unperturbed by its decrepit appearance. The fact that it was so smothered with overgrown brambles and shrubs that it could hardly by seen at a distance of three feet did not deter him. Neither did the state of the top deck which was covered with layers of rubbish and weeds; nor the interior which had long been 'home' to a variety of insects, small mammals, and a multifarious collection of articles including tins, bottles, lamps, paper and books — all covered with the mud, dust and cobwebs of many years.

Prince Marshall thought that the bus was worth restoring in spite of its wretched condition and strange resting-place, and he began negotiations with the trustees of the late owner. This proved to be a long drawn-out operation and it was late in 1971 before the vehicle could be moved to coachbuilders for complete restoration.

To rebuild such a dilapidated vehicle was a long job, but it was finished eventually and the Dennis was painted in the red livery of the old London General Omnibus Company and fitted with an exact replica of the destination and route board for Route 529. It then looked fresh and bright, and ready for an active life. Which was just as well, because Prince Marshall believes that old vehicles should be "made to work", that they deteriorate when "laid-up in museums", and he has pursued this policy with the 1925 Dennis.

It has been driven many thousands of miles to rallies and on publicity compaigns in Britain, and has also travelled overseas. Prince Marshall explained that in August 1972 the bus went to Yokohama and Tokyo, followed by a 3000-mile three-month publicity tour of Japan on behalf of the Department of Trade and Industry; and he added that the only problem throughout this marathon trip was "one dropped valve guide".

The publicity campaigns in Britain have been varied and included an extensive project for Baxters (Butchers) Ltd., during which children from schools in many towns were given rides; reports show that the open top deck was always popular — even in wet weather. Baxters also organised a competition for the best painting of the bus by a young child, and this was won by a pupil at Hungerford Primary School in Berkshire.

Numbers of pensioners have enjoyed riding in the vehicle — the more venturesome mounting to the top deck despite the somewhat intimidating open spiral staircase with tapered steps. In recent years a senior citizen has also been at the wheel, for the bus has been driven by Mr Bert Blower who was driving buses as long ago as the 1920's. In fact, he drove a 'pirate' bus in London during the tumultuous period of the independent bus companies.

This reliable old vehicle has undertaken many other activities. It has been used to advertise holidays in England for the English Tourist Board, and has made several television appearances, the most notable being episodes in the 'Father Brown' series and 'Upstairs Downstairs'. It was a particularly fine sight in the edition of 'Upstairs Downstairs' shown on Sunday 2nd November, 1975, when it was driven in scenes depicting the General Strike of 1926. This was a fitting role for the old vehicle since it is likely that it really was used for this purpose in 1926 when hundreds of independent buses continued to run in London — all operating from a temporary base in Regent's Park.

The 'Upstairs Downstairs' episode captured the atmosphere of the period when XX 9591 came to a halt with radiator steaming - a calamity that was intended to reflect the ineptitude of the amateur driver. Likewise, the brief altercation that followed between strikers, passengers and volunteer driver was shown, no doubt, to convey the strong feelings of those involved, for reports of the time mention bitter incidents in the capital and buses running with boarded windows.

This 1925 Dennis bus with its open spiral staircase was an attractive addition to the programme. There is little doubt that it will be in use for years to come; that many people will ride in it and many more will enjoy looking at it. To me, it represents the day of the independent or 'pirate' bus which was a time of tempestuous development and expansion in the evolution of public road transport.

It was also a time of great confusion. The licensing of passenger carrying vehicles was based on 19th century Acts of Parliament and controls were almost non-existent. In fact, the Road Traffic Act of 1930 was the first major legislation to control the licensing and operation of passenger carrying commercial vehicles. It was not, however, universally popular, and there is no doubt that some small operators were put out of business by measures introduced to limit the number of licences available for passenger carrying services. Yet regulations controlling the use and condition of passenger carrying vehicles were essential.

The Act was necessary. It brought order where there had been confusion — but the exciting and enterprising days of the independent bus companies had gone for ever.

Chapter Eight

Foden Steam Wagons of 1926 and 1929 Vintage
"But strong for service still, and unimpair'd".
Wm. Cowper.

The history of steam locomotion is a fusion of enterprise and solid function. In the early 1900's it reflected
the best aspects of British engineering skills, and its
role in the evolution of commercial road transport was
notable. Indeed, for a few years steam was more
popular than the internal combustion engine as a
means of heavy long-distance goods haulage.

Two great names at the pinnacle of steam wagon
development are Foden and Sentinel, and - like the
Sentinel 'steamer' described in chapter 13 — the two
Foden wagons featured here are robust examples of
the manufacturer's best work.

The Foden Company had been in existence for some
years when its first steam wagon was projected. It
was founded in the mid 1850's by Edwin Foden who
began on a small scale as a manufacturer of agricultural
machinery. He was later joined by his son William and
together they built up the Company which became
known for the development and manufacture of
agricultural traction engines. So, at the moment when
the efficient steam road vehicle became a reality the
Foden Company was already working in a related field
of engineering. Edwin and William were quick to
recognise this opportunity and to grasp it. The first
Foden 'road-steamer' was in production by the turn
of the century, and when the two 6-ton wagons of this

Rare and Interesting Commercial Vehicles

chapter were built in the 1920's E. Foden, Sons & Company Limited of Sandbach, Cheshire, was known throughout the world for the production of steam road vehicles.

Every 'steamer' was inspected and tested to the zenith degree before it left the Foden workshops. Yet the Company knew that the long-term success of each wagon depended upon the quality of driving and general maintenance that it would receive during its working life, and this was emphasised again and again in the Foden Wagon Driver's Instruction Manual. The opening paragraphs read:

> "The efficiency of the steam wagon depends entirely on the care and attention exercised by the driver, and his having moderate ideas of speed. In the hands of a skilful man — that is one who attends to thorough lubrication of every moving part, and to other points mentioned hereafter — a wagon will outlast at least six in the charge of a reckless and careless man.

> "We cannot impress too strongly on the owners of these wagons, that to get the best result, and to work the wagon at its highest money-making capacity, a good driver is essential."

The importance of a 'good driver' is referred to again a few pages later:

> "Always endeavour to drive the wagon as near as possible to the legal speed, stated on the near side girder. A driver with moderate ideas of speed gets over more ground than the so-called driver who races the engine for an hour and is then compelled to stop and repair some damage. When nearing an incline test the brakes to see that they are working properly, and when descending go carefully, so that you can stop the wagon in case of emergency."

68

PLATE 14—1926 Foden Steam Wagon

Owner: H. E. Parkin & Son

PLATE 15—1929 Foden Steam Wagon collecting 2,000 bricks from Ockley Brickworks
in Sussex

Owner: Denis Brandt

Photo: Bill Mackenzie

Foden Steam Wagons of 1926 & 1929 Vintage

Several pages are filled with useful instructions for the maintenance of Foden steam wagons. The driver is told that "while steam is being raised" he should give the engine "a good cleaning", and at the same time should "keep a good look out for loose nuts, missing split pins, etc.". It is sensibly pointed out that "the man who never cleans his engine seldom finds anything wrong until he gets a smash up".

Considerable instruction on the care of the boiler is given, the driver being advised that this vital item should be washed out every week, and that "under no circumstances should it be worked without a thorough cleaning".

Certainly the owner of a new Foden 'steamer' assumed that his vehicle would be capable of hard, heavy work for a long time to come, and if he exercised the care outlined in the Driver's Manual he was rarely disappointed. The two wagons described here were, undoubtedly, alike in giving years and years of service. They were also alike in having several owners, and in belonging to the same owner at the same time for a few years in the early 1950's when they were both used for tar-spraying.

Tar-spraying became a popular occupation for heavy wagons because, as road-making machines on contract to public authorities, they were not subject to the vicious taxation that began to penalise heavy road vehicles in the 1930's. However, this is to look ahead; the effects of such punitive fiscal measures were not evident when these two 6-ton 'steamers' were new.

The first of the two wagons left the Foden works on 8th July, 1926, and Mr A. V. Evans of Fodens has given me a copy of the original work-sheet which contains this date. Many technical details are also given, and the following are taken from the boiler section:

Boiler type	...	6 ton.
Boiler diameter	...	2' 2"
Number of tubes	...	63 — fire. 3 — stay.
Class of tubes	...	Howell 13G.
Tubed by	...	656 (presumably this was the engineer's workshop number).
Hydraulic test to	...	380 lbs.
Test witnessed by	...	H. Barlow (Foreman).
Date of test	...	14th May, 1926.

The Foden work-sheet records the fact that Mr E. B. Devenish, Haulage Contractor of Rayleigh in Essex, was the first owner of the wagon. This is confirmed on the original logbook (now held by the present owner of the wagon) which also provides the information that the 'steamer' was registered for the first time on the 30th June, 1926, and given registration number TW 4207.

The Devenish Company still exists and still operates in Rayleigh. Mr J. B. Devenish told me recently that the old Foden is remembered in his Company despite the passing of more than 50 years. He explained that it was used "for general cartage from Rayleigh Goods Depot on contract for the London & North Eastern Railway to local farms etc.".

There was a change of ownership in 1927 when the vehicle was acquired by Mr H. A. Stutley of Stevenage, Hertfordshire. Mr Stutley's son has told the present owner that his father bought the wagon through

Scammel & Nephew of Spitalfields, London for £810. The 'steamer' was used in H. A. Stutley's sand and gravel business for almost eight years, and it is thought that it was converted to a three-way tipper during this period. Mr Stutley sold the vehicle to Mr Ernest H. Wyatt of Buntingford, Hertfordshire, in April 1935.

Ernest Wyatt still remembers the wagon, and in a letter written in May 1978 he explains that he used it for "steaming tanks of tar at Buntingford Station during 1935". He goes on to say that although he sold the vehicle to Taroads Limited of Finsbury Circus, London, in March 1936, he remained connected with it. In fact, he helped to fit a tank and spraying gear to the wagon, and then drove it for Taroads on tar-spraying operations in Hertfordshire during the summer of 1936. Mr Wyatt lost sight of TW 4207 in 1937 when the Company moved it to another depot; but he had not seen the last of the vehicle, for he was to come across it once more — many years later.

Taroads used the 'steamer' for tar-spraying and associated road-work from 1937 until it was transferred to Northern Taroads Limited of Kendal, Westmorland, during August 1948. Here too it was used for road-building, and when Northern Taroads acquired the other Foden 'steamer' of this chapter in 1950, both vehicles operated out of the same yard on road-making activities for a few years.

In February 1959 Northern Taroads sold TW 4207 to D. Wood & Company of Leeds. At this date the vehicle was 33 years of age; but it was still capable of steaming its way through a day's work and was sent to the Wood Company's yard at Hormby Quarry, Leyburn in North Yorkshire. Two years of use followed, and in 1961 the Company decided that the elderly wagon's commercial life had come to an end.

TW 4207 was then taken out of service having been at

work for 35 years; 35 years of heavy work for many
owners, and in many parts of the country. A fine
record.

The wagon remained at Leyburn after its retirement,
and when the Wood Company was taken over by a
group organisation in 1962 it was relegated to the
status of 'scrap'. Therefore when a purge of out-of-
date machinery and vehicles was begun in 1963 it was
decided that the 1926 'steamer' would be cut up —
and this would have been its end if someone who cares
about smoky, snorting old steam wagons had not
thought otherwise.

Mr Harry Parkin of Cutsyke, Castleford, has tremendous enthusiasm for the fine old 'road-steamers' of
the 1920's and he already knew of TW 4207. Thus,
when he heard of the vehicle's imminent demise he
contacted the Company and made an offer immediately. Within 24 hours of this being accepted, Harry
Parkin had borrowed a wagon and towed the old Foden
'steamer' the 60 miles from Hormby Quarry, Leyburn,
to his home in West Yorkshire.

On the following day (20th June 1963) Mr Parkin and
his son, David, spent time inspecting the 6-tonner, and
they came to the conclusion that, despite its well worn
condition, it was still capable of being steamed. There-
upon the vehicle was steamed and, in David Parkin's
words, it "was taken for a short run round local lanes
and performed adequately"; which was a notable feat
after 35 years of hard work, followed by two years of
complete idleness. The Parkins were delighted with
their new acquisition and, there and then, christened it
"Tiny".

The success of the 'short run' convinced Harry and
David that their 1926 Foden could be restored to peak
performance, and this has been done in gradual stages
and over several years. The work has included the

removal of the large tank on the back and replacement with a flat body; the reconditioning of boiler and engine, and the renovation of bodywork where necessary. In 1976 the boiler was re-tubed, and during the winter of 1977 the wagon was painted signal red and high-lighted with black lines.

In the early months of 1978 the vehicle was sign-written in gold leaf. The wording chosen was H. E. Parkin & Son to reflect the interest of the whole family —for Mrs Edna Parkin is as enthusiastic about "Tiny" as are her husband and son. It now remains to find and fit a tipper ram, and David Parkin explained that in the past the wagon was fitted with an hydraulic ram that "worked with water, not with oil as is usual".

The Parkins have now owned this 'steamer' for 15 years. Throughout these years they have worked on it and they have used it. In fact, the wagon was steamed to its first rally as early as August 1963, and in a recent letter David Parkin said that it was "steamed to every rally and show it attended between 1963 and 1976". During these years the vehicle travelled in Yorkshire, Nottinghamshire, Leicestershire and Lincolnshire. It was at a rally at Stamford, Lincolnshire, in the early 1970's that Ernest Wyatt saw the old Foden and he recognised it at once — despite the passing of almost 40 years.

Driving their 6-tonner to so many events, and for so many miles, has resulted in 'long hours' for Harry and David Parkin because their work commitments do not allow them to start off on week-end rallies until Friday evenings. Therefore, they were glad to acquire a Foden low-loader which they immediately named 'Tiny Tim', and this vehicle was used to take TW 4207 to Battersea on 7th May, 1978 for its first Historic Commercial Vehicle Club London to Brighton Run.

When the Parkin wagon arrived at Battersea for the

'start' of the Run it was joined by the 1929 Foden that had worked with it in Westmorland many years before. The two wagons made a fine sight as they 'steamed' off together for the Brighton Road.

It is likely that the 1978 London to Brighton Run will always be memorable for Harry and David Parkin because 'Tiny' was the first 'steamer' to reach Brighton and was awarded third prize in the Steam Wagon and Tractor class. The vehicle's requirements during the Run were 2½ cwts of coal and 160 gallons of water — the water consumption being particularly convenient as its tank capacity is 180 gallons.

The second Foden wagon of this chapter left the Company's workshops in 1929, and details taken from the boiler section of the Foden work-sheet show that it had many features in common with its colleague of 1926 vintage:

Boiler type	...	6 ton.
Boiler diameter	...	2' 2".
Number of tubes	...	66 — fire.
		Nil — stay.
Class of tubes	...	Howell.
Hydraulic test to	...	380 lbs.
Test witnessed by	...	H. Barlow (foreman).
Date of test	...	26th July, 1929.
Tubed by	...	656

Readers will notice that both Fodens were tubed by '656' and that H. Barlow witnessed the hydraulic test on each wagon.

The Foden work-sheet also provides the information that the first owner of the vehicle was Samuel Kidd & Co. Ltd., flour millers of Hertfordshire, and it is disappointing that it has not been possible to confirm the length of time that the wagon remained with this firm.

It is, however, known that it was registered RO 6330 and was owned by the Roadway Portland Cement Company of Dunstable, Bedfordshire, in the late 1930's.

Taroads Limited of London acquired RO 6330 in 1943 and it operated from the Company's Highgate depot for some years. It was converted for tar-spraying during this period. In 1950 the vehicle was transferred to Northern Taroads of Kendal, Westmorland where it was used on road-making operations in company with the 1926 Foden TW 4207.

RO 6330 had several owners in the next ten years, including John A. Clayton of Conisbrough, Arthur Gosney of Sheffield and Peter Harper of Stretton, Cheshire.

It was approximately nine years ago when John Clayton became the owner, and he too carried out substantial work on the 1929 'steamer'. In a letter written in June 1978 he gave details of this work which included the fitting of:

> "One new gearbox shaft.
> Wheel studs (40 in all).
> Front Mudguards."

John Clayton's letter continues:

> "I had the cab re-built and body made in Bawtry, also a new door fitted in the back of the cab to make fire mending easier.

> "The plate (The Foden Steam Wagon) I had cast in brass by Fodens."

When the work was finished John Clayton took the wagon out on two or three trial runs, and he was disconcerted to find that he had difficulty in getting steam up on every occasion. As he could not rectify this fault he sold the vehicle back to Mr Arthur Gosney from whom he had bought it.

In 1971 RO 6330 came into the ownership of Mr Peter Harper who carried out useful work on the boiler; but the future of this old 'steamer' was uncertain until 1972 when Peter Harper sold it to Mr Denis Brandt.

When Mr Brandt acquired the wagon in the summer of 1972 it was, to use his words, "by no means in a dilapidated state". He referred to its condition as "rather scruffy" and said that there had been a mechanical accident on the high pressure side of the engine with the result that a connecting rod on that side had become slightly bent. Denis Brandt decided that all the renovation necessary to return the Foden to good order should be executed by a team of experts in Lancashire. He described the work that was carried out in the following manner:

> "The problem on the H.P. side was dealt with and the engine generally tidied up. The body and cab were removed so that work could be done to the chassis, and the back of the cab was re-built. Apart from filling, rubbing, painting and lining out, no other major repair was necessary."

This work was done under Mr Brandt's instructions during the period September 1972 to March 1973, and he was delighted to be able to commence rallying the Foden in April 1973. After twenty years of idleness and uncertainty RO 6330 was once more in 'top gear'.

The wagon is now parked at the Kew Bridge Pumping Station which has been its home since Denis Brandt made contact with the group of enthusiasts who

PLATE 16—1926 and 1929 Foden Steam Wagons—during the 1978 London to Brighton Run

PLATE 17—1926 W. & G. Du Cross Ambulance

Owner: London Ambulance Service

Photo: Greater London Council
Photographic Unit

Foden Steam Wagons of 1926 and 1929 Vintage

restored the Kew Bridge Pumping Engines and turned the Station into what he describes as "London's only living steam museum".

"London's only living steam museum" is an ideal parking place for the 1929 Foden. The vehicle is representative of, both the period when the manufacture of heavy steam vehicles reached the pinnacle of excellence, and of the moment when this form of road transport was about to be annihilated by the development of the diesel-engined lorry. A notable point of time in industrial history.

Clearly, RO 6330 and the Pumping Station project were on the same 'wave-length', and Denis Brandt was glad to be able to use his Foden to help with the work. For example, he mentioned an occasion when he drove the wagon to collect four tons of bricks from the Ockley Brick Works in Sussex — the brick company having offered the bricks free-of-charge provided that they were collected by a steam vehicle. When the bricks reached Kew they were used for "building up around a Lancashire boiler".

Since returning to the rally scene in 1973 this 49-year-old wagon has been active in many ways. It has helped with the pumping station project, it has been steamed to shows and rallies, and it has taken part in the annual Historic Commercial Vehicle Club's London to Brighton Run when it met up with its erstwhile mate of Westmorland days.

As these two wagons moved off together at the start of the Run they evoked not only the distant era of the massive 'road-steamer', but also the name of one of the few firms that has found the way to adjust and grow through many decades of change in the heavy commercial road vehicle industry.

When the Foden Company built TW 4207 and RO 6330 it had already been established for about 70 years, and it operates today—50 years later. This remarkable achievement is due in great measure to the foresight of William Foden who made the important decision to take the Company into the production of diesel lorries at the end of the 1920's. The first Foden diesel-engined lorry was ready for launching in 1931 and the Company has maintained its position in world markets ever since.

Today, the Foden Company is fighting for an even bigger share of United Kingdom markets, and is proving to be a powerful competitor of Scandinavian truck manufacturers, such as Volvo and Scania, who held about 30% of U.K. sales of heavy lorries in 1978.

Perhaps this progression has been possible because the members of the Foden family have always been able to comprehend and accomplish the changes necessary to maintain a buoyant industrial operation; and this remains so in 1978. At the present time Messrs W. L. Foden, D. C. Foden, E. S. Foden and S. P. Tremlow are senior directors of the Company as well as great grandsons of Edwin Foden, the founder — Mr Tremlow's grandfather having married Miss Fanny Foden. Family achievements of this magnitude are becoming rarer and it would, surely, be a satisfaction to Edwin Foden to know that his lineal descendants are at the head of the business he founded so many years ago.

Following are the specifications of the two vehicles chronicled in this chapter:

1926 6-Ton Foden Steam Wagon __ TW 4207

Maker's number	12364
Length	22 feet overall (body 12 feet).
Width	8 feet across widest point (rear axle).

Foden Steam Wagons of 1926 and 1929 Vintage

Working Pressure	225 P.S.I.
Type of engine	Compound (Double Crank).
Number of cylinders	Two
Cylinder bore	High pressure 4¼" Low pressure 7".
Piston stroke	Approx. 7".
Unladen weight	6 tons 15 cwt.
Pay load — wagon	6 tons.
Pay load — trailer	Depending on trailer type approx. 4 to 6 tons.
Water tank capacity	180 gallons.
Type of fuel	Coal or coke (preferably Welsh steam coal — smokeless).
Fuel consumption	e.g. London/Brighton 53 miles 2½ cwt.
Water consumption	e.g. London/Brighton 160 gallons.
Top speed today	25 — 30 m.p.h. capable speed. maximum speed not known.
Body type	Replica of box type for three-way tipping.
Colour	Chocolate originally. Now red.

Specification details provided by David Parkin.

1929 6-Ton Foden Steam Wagon —RO 6330

Maker's number	13488

Length	21 feet
Width	7 feet 9 inches.
Working pressure	220 P.S.I.
Type of engine	Compound
Number of cylinders	Two
Cylinder bore	High pressure 4½" Low pressure 7".
Piston stroke	7"
Unladen weight	5 ton 14 cwt.
Pay load — wagon	6 tons
Pay load — trailer	10 tons
Water tank capacity	180 gallons
Type of fuel	Coal
Fuel consumption	12-15 miles per cwt.
Water consumption	4 gallons per mile.
Top speed today	25-30 miles per hour.
Body type	Dropside.
Colour	Blue.

Specification details provided by **Denis Brandt.**

PLATE 18—1935 Talbot Ambulance

Owner: London Ambulance Service   *Photo*: Greater London Council
Photographic Unit

Owner: Nick Baldwin

PLATE 19—1929 Bean 30-Cwt Lorry

Photo: J. R. Smith

Chapter Nine

*London Ambulance Service Vehicles
1926 Du Cross and 1935 Talbot*

Progress, therefore, is not an accident, but a necessity.
Herbert Spencer.

Organised ambulance services were surprisingly slow
to emerge. From time to time some sort of service
would be set up to cope with an epidemic and would
fade away when the outbreak began to die out. The
need for a regular service to transport the sick was not
recognised until the 19th century, and even then it was
only thought necessary for infectious patients.

The situation was most acute in London where the
number of cases of smallpox, cholera and fever increased with the growth of the population. In the early
1800's responsibility for the movement of infectious
patients was devolved upon 30 separate Boards of
Guardians of the Poor; but despite the number of such
Boards, or perhaps because of it, little progress was
made. The first step forward came with the introduction of the Metropolitan Poor Act, 1867, and the re-
sulting formation of the Metropolitan Asylums Board.
The MAB met for the first time on 22nd June, 1867,
and within months had provided hospitals for smallpox and fever cases, as well as institutions for mental
defectives. In addition, the Board provided a horse-
drawn ambulance to convey infectious patients to its
own hospitals.

A History of the Metropolitan Asylums Board,
written by Sir Allan Powell and published in 1930,
describes the disastrous arrangements that existed for

the movement of infectious persons before the Board came into being. Sir Allan explains, for example, that "it was not unusual for sufferers from infectious diseases to travel to hospital in public vehicles to the common danger", and he goes on to say that in instances when a private carriage was hired to remove a smallpox or fever case it was likely that, having delivered the patient, the carriage would be parked in a yard surrounded by tradesmens' carts.

In another paragraph Sir Allan says:

> "Frequent complaints were made of the carriages conveying patients to hospitals stopping at public houses into which the driver and the patient's friends went for refreshment."

Certainly there was cause for concern, and as the 1800's progressed there was a growing realisation of the dangers of transporting infectious persons in public vehicles. In 1886 the Commissioner of Police asked the Metropolitan Asylums Board to "undertake the disinfection of public carriages that had been so used"; but, as Sir Allan explains in his history, the Board declined to take on this work ".... on the ground that owing to the furniture of these carriages complete disinfection was impossible". The Board, however, made representations which led to the introduction of the Poor Law Act, 1889. This Act gave the MAB authority to remove "in its own ambulances persons to other places than the Board's hospitals".

Rapid improvement in the movement of infectious patients soon followed. Yet there were no ambulances for the transport of victims of street accidents or sudden illnesses. Such persons were lucky if they were conveyed to hospitals or workhouse infirmaries in horse-drawn carriages or carts; others might be taken on police hand- or wheeled-litters which were comprised principally of two poles and a piece of cloth. Some sufferers managed to struggle to hospitals on foot with the support of friends, and some never arrived. To what extent a patient's condition was aggravated by his journey to hospital was not considered.

The number of street accidents and other casualties increased noticeably as the 20th century dawned, and in 1904 the medical profession, which hitherto had shown no interest in the provision of ambulance services, began to urge the setting-up of a unified system. The profession as a body recommended that an integrated ambulance service should be based on hospitals and operated by the London County Council.

In response to this recommendation the London County Council attempted to set up a unified ambulance service in the London area in 1906, but failed to obtain permission from H.M. Government on the grounds that it would be too costly. Discussions were suggested and a committee comprised of officials of the LCC and the Home Office was formed. Committees, however, are slow to reach decisions and even slower to act; and in 1907 the City of London decided to launch its own ambulance service.

A history of the development of ambulance services in the metropolis published by the London Ambulance Service explains that the new service made a useful start:

"......One electric ambulance was bought, and then another two when a second station was opened. They operated a 24-hour service and could be called by telephone from 52 street call boxes."

The committee meanwhile continued its deliberations and in 1909 issued a report. The History published by the L.A.S. continues:

> "In 1909 the committee reported that the existing service was unsatisfactory and that the Metropolitan Asylums Board should operate a unified service. (Street accidents had, incidentally, increased by 60 per cent while the committee was sitting). This was opposed and a Bill was passed giving the London County Council power to run **an accident service** independently of the Metropolitan Asylums Board. This new service opened in February 1915 under the control of the Chief Officer of the Fire Brigade."

From 1915 to 1930 the ambulance services of the Metropolitan Asylums Board and the London County Council operated independently on their respective types of work. These were years of growth for both authorities. The MAB, for example, greatly extended the number of its hospitals and institutions, and when the first vehicle of this chapter was new in 1926, the Board had become the largest user of civilian ambulances in the world.

The MAB designed its own ambulances to meet a variety of specialised needs, and the 1926 Du Cross vehicle featured here was designed by the Board's engineering superintendent. It was built on a 'Meadows' chassis by William and George Du Cross of Fulham and registered YT 9792. The vehicle's measurements are body 16' 10", width 6' 4" and height 7' 2". It wears a grey livery with 1" black band all round and has the MAB badge on the front of the radiator shell. The final appearance is nicely set-off with brass headlamps.

London Ambulance Service Vehicles

YT 9792 became the property of the London County Council in 1930 when the introduction of the Local Government Act, 1929, brought into being a unified ambulance service. This Act contained a measure to abolish the Boards of Guardians of the Poor and to transfer the duties of the Metropolitan Asylums Board to the London County Council thereby creating the integrated ambulance service that had been recommended in 1904.

At the time of the transfer the London Ambulance Service was operating 14 stations with 20 ambulances and a staff of 165. When it took over six large stations, 107 vehicles and a staff of 270 from the MAB it became a large authority, and it was soon evident that the work of the Service was being hampered by the multiplicity of ambulance vehicles that made up its working fleet. Some uniformity of vehicle was essential, and a Talbot ambulance was purpose-designed and introduced gradually throughout the Service.

The Talbot ambulance of this chapter was registered BXH 809 and brought into service in 1935. It has a body length of 17' 9", width 6' 4" and height 7' 6". The vehicle's blue and white "Accident Ambulance" sign, and its white livery with black wings and lining effectively create the comforting appearance of a conventional ambulance.

Both the Du Cross ambulance and the Talbot are preserved by the London Ambulance Service** and I am indebted to the Chief Officer, Mr T. R. Walton, for the information he has given me.

It is significant that the two vehicles described here were purpose-built for ambulance work and that each, in its period, represented a step forward in the development of this vital service.

**The Ambulance Services of the London County Council and three Regional Health Authorities were formed into the London Ambulance Service in 1965.

Rare and Interesting Commercial Vehicles

Specification details are:

1926 W. & G. Du Cross Ambulance __ YT 9792

Engine	3½ litres (2600 c.c.)
Cylinders	6
Gearbox	Crash, 4 forward, 1 reverse
Maximum m.p.h.	About 40 m.p.h.
Type of fuel	Petrol
Seating capacity	1 stretcher plus escort. Crew of 3

1935 Talbot Ambulance — BXH 809

Engine	2.9 litres (27 h.p.)
Cylinders	6
Gearbox	Preselector
Maximum m.p.h.	About 40 m.p.h.
Type of fuel	Petrol
Seating capacity	2 stretchers

Specification details provided by T.R. Walton.

Chapter Ten

1929 Bean 30-cwt Lorry
A Sturdy Worker

It is noticeable that many of the vehicles chronicled
here have given years and years of service — not least
the Bean lorry of this chapter. It was built at the end of
1929 and was hauling coal from early 1932 until its
owner retired in 1959. Even then it could have gone on
had there been anyone else in the coal depot who could
cope with its right-hand crash gear change, centre
accelerator pedal and awkward hand start.

Almost 30 years of hard toil is a worthy achievement
and Nick Baldwin, who is the present owner of the
vehicle, believes it to be one of the longest working
lorries in the United Kingdom. This is a record that
speaks well for the manufacturers of Bean lorries.

The history of the Bean Company appears to be
compounded of sound work and adverse circumstances.
It was well established as a supplier of motor components in 1919 when the management decided to enter the
field of mass-produced cars and later to introduce a
truck range. This venture was successful in the early
days, but competition from Morris Motors and big
American manufacturers, such as Ford and Dodge, was
fierce as the 1920's advanced. The Bean Company's
answer to competition was to reduce the selling price of
its vehicles, and the 30-cwt lorry — which sold at £325
in 1929 — had been reduced to £198 by 1931. But this
was no answer. The profit margin was too low, and

87

competition, coupled with the effects of the 'slump', soon proved disastrous. The Company was forced to abandon the manufacture of motor vehicles.

Thus ended Bean Cars — a firm that began with high hopes and flourished for a few years. Happily, it was reformed in due course and once again supplied components to the motor industry.

It is thought that several thousand Bean lorries were built, but only a handful have survived, and a number of these are in Australia which was the Bean Company's best export market. Therefore, Nick Baldwin's vehicle is a rarity. Indeed, he believes it to be the only restored example of the Company's final 30-cwt flat truck model, and it still bears the wording 'Bean Cars Ltd. Tipton' beneath the driver's door.

Nick Baldwin explained that this lorry began life as a demonstration model for a Bean dealer in Redditch. It was then sold to Alfred Manssuer of Stratford-on-Avon who used it for almost 30 years to deliver coal to homes in the Stratford area and to Flower's Brewery for the brewery's fleet of steam wagons. In addition, the vehicle made journeys to and from the annual Stratford Mop carrying coal for the showmen's engines.

In later years Mr Manssuer used a modern lorry when he wished to impress important customers; but he kept the old Bean in use on the coal-round. In fact, the present owner has been told that the vehicle was often over-loaded and could be seen struggling up Sunrising Hill (1 in 7) carrying as much as 50 hundredweights of bagged coal. Yet it was always well maintained, and was in working order when the owner retired at the end of the 1950's.

Mr Baldwin is joint editor of *Old Motor* and his enthusiasm for aged commercial vehicles is of longstanding. He wanted to own this old Bean as far back as the early 1950's when he first spotted it; and his opinion did not change when he saw it occasionally in the following years. It was always at work on the coal-round and was, he says, "a most incongruous sight". At that time Nick Baldwin knew nothing of the vehicle's history, and his efforts to trace the owner were thwarted by the lorry being always on the move and the name and address on the side panels having become too faded to read. He was still making enquiries when the vehicle disappeared in 1960.

Several years passed before Nick was able to get news of the Bean and then he heard, on what he calls "the old-vehicle network", that it was in the country some miles from Stratford. He learned that it belonged to Mr Alfred Manssuer who had sent the vehicle to the country when he retired in 1960 and could not park it at his home in a residential district of Stratford-on-Avon. When the two men met Mr Manssuer explained that he had bought the Bean from a dealer in Redditch, and was, therefore, its first and only owner. This was good news and Nick Baldwin was delighted — that is until Alfred Manssuer added that the old lorry was about to be cut up and made into a farm trailer.

Swift action was called for, and within a few days Nick had seen the lorry, made an offer (despite the shock of its dilapidated appearance) and achieved his ambition to become the owner of a rare Bean truck.

Certainly, the appearance of his new acquisition was grim, and in an article written later Nick explained that the Bean had "deteriorated rapidly after its owner's retirement". He went on:

"......it had stood in the open in the country for years, being a great favourite with the local children, who managed to fill every available cranny, including the petrol tank and radiator, with sand. The final straw was when a well-meaning farmer towed it into a barn, only to have the roof collapse on it in the winter!"

Rare and Interesting Commercial Vehicles

Fortunately the ramshackle appearance of the vehicle did not daunt its new owner, and after removing about two feet of dry rot from the platform and eradicating rot and rust holes in the timber and steel cab he was pleased to find that it was completely original. The necessary mechanical work included new fibre couplings in the transmission, overhauling of the electrics and carburettor, and a re-bushed gear-lever. A new radiator was required, and after fruitless efforts to find one, Mr Baldwin overcame the problem by contacting a friend at Chelsea School of Art who sculptured a new top tank for the radiator, using the 'lost wax' process.

The restored lorry is still original, in fact the owner describes it as refurbished rather than restored; but it was some years before it reached this stage. Nick Baldwin was unable to commence the restoration before 1968, and it then occupied his free time for a further two years. So it was 1970 before the work was finished and the old Bean was ready to take part in its first Historic Commercial Vehicle Club London to Brighton Run.

This was the Bean's first journey for ten years and it performed well. Nick Baldwin says that it "never missed a beat in 300 miles, used no oil, returned a steady 15 miles to the gallon and won a cup for the best restoration by an a owner of limited means", or as he put it "an impoverished owner ". Since that time the lorry has taken part in rallies and subsequent London-Brighton Runs, and has always performed satisfactorily.

At the time of writing (November '77) the old Bean is being used by Southern BRS on a promotional exercise and is painted in BRS orange and white livery. British Road Services have carried out mechanical work on the lorry, and when Nick drove it recently it reached 40 m.p.h. with little effort. Even then it was not 'flat out',

90

but he did not attempt to increase speed because the braking system is not up to the standard required in present-day traffic.

As with many vehicles of the period the Bean has only rear wheel brakes. Hand brake shoes and foot brake shoes operate in the same brake drums, with the result that should the drums become over-heated while applying the foot brake when descending a steep hill it is of little use to apply the hand brake to over-heated drums.

Today, this rare Bean lorry is almost 50 years of age and, having escaped destruction by a hair's breadth in 1965, is all set to go on for another 50 years.

Brief specification details are:

Horse power	13.9 h.p.
Cylinders	Four
Fuel	Petrol
Fuel consumption	15 m.p.g.
Top speed	50 m.p.h. (when new)
Load capacity	30 cwt.

Chapter Eleven

1929 Dennis 30-cwt Platform Truck
A Useful Servant

Years of useful work, air raid damage followed by more work, neglect, restoration and historic status are all part of the history of this Dennis platform truck; part of a history that began in 1929 when the vehicle was bought new by Fowlers Forest Dairies Ltd., of Sparkhill, Birmingham. It was registered UW 9679, and used to collect milk from farms south of Birmingham — the majority being in the Henley-in-Arden area where churns of milk were collected from about 16 farms and taken to Sparkhill for processing and retailing.

The Fowler Company was founded as long ago as 1898 by Mr John Fowler, and it was his son James who bought the truck. In fact, he purchased two identical 30-cwt vehicles at the time, and he remembered both in October 1975 when he described them as "exceptionally reliable" and praised the Dennis worm-driven rear axle which he said was a notable feature. James Fowler's son, David, also remembers the old vehicles and he spoke of days in his youth when he was allowed to ride with the driver of UW 9679. He explained that these were exciting occasions, especially when the driver had to have "two or three goes at steep hills", usually coming to a halt midway and returning to the beginning to make another attempt.

UW 9679 gave many years of good service. Indeed, it continued in use after it had been damaged in an air raid during the Second World War and fitted with a somewhat 'utility' cab as a result. James Fowler believes that the vehicle was on the road until about 1947, and that it was withdrawn from service because of poor brakes — these being on the rear wheels only.

The truck was then used for a while on odd jobs about the farm, before being laid-up under a hedge in a field at the back of the farmhouse. It was still there in 1970 when it was seen by Mr Paul Peacock of Bromsgrove.

Clearly, the lorry was in poor condition after such a long period in the open. It looked, in fact, like a candidate for the scrap yard when Mr Peacock came along, and it is fortunate that he recognised its historical significance. Paul Peacock hoped to restore the old Dennis, but when a couple of years had passed and he had not been able to make a start he decided to sell the vehicle and advertised it in a motoring magazine.

His advertisement was seen by Clive Peerless of Newton Longville, Buckinghamshire, who had been looking for just such a vehicle for sometime. Mr Peerless was very tempted, but the asking price was more than he could afford and he did not go to see the Dennis until it was advertised at a lower price some months later. Then his first sight of the 1929 vehicle came as something of a shock, for the deterioration was greater than expected; but the price was reasonable and as it was so exactly what he wanted he made the purchase.

The new owner was then faced with the problem of transporting the truck to his home, and this was overcome in February, 1974, when a sympathetic friend offered the use of his Landrover and trailer. The journey proved to be difficult, and Clive was glad to have the company of Mr Brian Brown who subsequently helped him with the restoration. Together they coped with icy roads, fog, and three punctured tyres on the trailer. When they finally reached Newton Longville the Dennis was parked in Mr Peerless's moderately-sized front garden, where it remained for many months while the rebuilding was carried out — an arrangement that says much for the good nature of his family and neighbours.

Clive Peerless had checked the condition of the vintage Dennis before purchasing and he knew what work had to be done. He also knew what items had to be replaced and these, he told me, included the radiator, carburettor, bonnet, dynamo and front mudguards. He explained that the vehicle had to be stripped down to the chassis as this was badly rusted, and that it was necessary to cut four feet off each side of the front of the chassis and weld in new sections; this last operation being undertaken by a friend with expertise in welding.

In addition the war-time cab — which Brian Brown described as "a horrible looking thing" — had to be scrapped, and a new cab built from photographs and drawings available to Mr Peerless.

The restoration was a long job, the more so as it had to be done in the open, thereby limiting much of the working time to week-ends. But the two men had a target to work for. It was their ambition to enter and complete the Historic Commercial Vehicle Club's annual London to Brighton Run on 6th May, 1975.

Somehow the work was finished by May 6th, and the vehicle was running quite well when Clive and Brian set off from Newton Longville — cheered on their way by a surprisingly large party of friends and neighbours who had gathered to wish them well. But it soon became embarrassingly evident that all was not well, and with no more than four miles on the clock the engine spluttered and died. Then followed several hours of hard work and frustration by the roadside before Clive Peerless decided to "give-up", and the smart commercial vehicle gleaming with newly-applied bright green paint had to be towed back to his home and once more parked outside his front door.

Both men were bitterly disappointed, but after further hours of work they had the Dennis in running order again and have since referred to the set-back as "just one of those unfortunate things".

In the years since 1975 the vehicle has been sign-written and fitted with sides. It has entered many rallies and been seen in shows and exhibitions for charity. In 1977 it completed the London/Brighton Run successfully and achieved an award in its class. It was also successful in the Trans-Pennine Run in the same year.

When I saw the truck it was bedded-down for the winter in a barn at Stewkley. But this did not worry Clive Peerless who soon had it out and running, and I noticed that the engine fired on the first attempt.

Today, this compact, practical-looking commercial vehicle does 15/16 miles to a gallon of petrol and has an average speed of 25 m.p.h., which is very fair as the Dennis 30-cwt chassis was not built for high speeds. Indeed, the Dennis Company's handbook for the model emphasised the importance of driving at moderate speeds:

> "**Excessive Speed.** We consider that, to obtain the best results with a Motor Vehicle, ample time should be allowed for the journeys to be undertaken, so that excessive road speed can be avoided. The vehicle will probably run a long time without showing much sign of ill-use, but it is certain that excessive speed on the road has to be paid for dearly in the end."

As with all Dennis Company manuals, this handbook gave a vast amount of information and provided an extensive list of things that should *not* be done i.e. "Don'ts", including the injunction:

"Do not forget to switch on."

UW 9679 will be "switched on" many times in the future, for this 1929 truck is now set fair for more years of useful activity.

Specification details:

Engine	19.4 h.p.
Number of cylinders	Four
Bore	85 mm
Stroke	120 mm
Gearbox	Crash box with 4 forward gears and reverse.
Brakes	Rear wheel only — rod operated.
Maximum speed	30 m.p.h.
Type of fuel	Petrol
Fuel consumption	12 — 16 m.p.g.

PLATE 20—1929 Dennis 30-Cwt Platform Truck before restoration

Owner and Photo: Clive Peerless

PLATE 21—1929 Dennis 30-Cwt Platform Truck after restoration

Owner: Clive Peerless

Chapter Twelve

1930 Morris-Commercial Six-Wheeler 'D' Type
A Strong 'Climber'

In its day the Morris-Commercial Six-Wheeler 'D' type 6x4 met all the criteria necessary for a medium-weight lorry. It was powerful, reliable, and capable of prolonged hard work. In addition it was adaptable. The chassis was used for ambulances, fire engines, mobile workshops, troop carriers and other special-ised purposes — as well as for the basic role of a lorry able to carry substantial loads on roads and cross country.

From the beginning the 'D' type was associated with military usage, and this is highlighted by Harry Edwards in an article in the *Journal of the Morris Register* (summer 1972 Vol. 6, No. 6). Mr Edwards points out that during his researches it became obvious "that the vehicle was designed with military uses and the 'Subsidy' scheme in mind". He explains that the Subsidy scheme was introduced "quite early in the 20th century", in fact, "as soon as the War Office realised that there would be need for a large number of motor vehicles in the event of war", and he continues:

"......it was desirable, from a point of view of driver training and repairs, for this transport to be of a standard type. The problem was solved by a system of payments to owners of motor fleets whose vehicles were manufactured in accordance with specifications laid down by the War Office, thus ensuring a large pool of suitable vehicles which could be commandeered by the military in time of emergency."

War Office specifications were issued from time to time, and Harry Edwards adds that in the late 1920's the purchasers of subsidy-earning lorries received £120 per vehicle — this being paid in six half-yearly instalments of £20 each.

Manufacturers of medium and heavy goods vehicles were quick to realise the advantages of building to meet these specifications, and Morris Commercial Cars launched its 'D' type Six-Wheeler in the autumn of 1926. The vehicle qualified for subsidy under War Office Specification number 30 for a "Medium W.D. type Six-Wheeler Lorry".

The Morris-Commercial 'D' type was a conventional commercial six-wheeler lorry with the addition of a second back axle. With an overall gear reduction of 80:1 it had extraordinary climbing ability; and it may have been this factor that made the model attractive to both civilian and military users. It was fortunate to qualify under the Subsidy scheme and to be purchased direct by the Services. Admiralty and Air Ministry sources bought the 'D' type direct, and it was purchased in considerable numbers to equip the Indian Army and several British Regiments.

Civilian users were likewise attracted to the model and it sold well at home and abroad. Its successes overseas were referred to in an issue of *'Move'* (*Vol. 2, No. 3*) which is the official publication of the Commercial Vehicle and Road Transport Club:

1930 Morris-Commercial Six-Wheeler 'D' Type

"The new model proved to be exceptionally sturdy, versatile and reliable, and was exported in large numbers to countries such as Norway, Egypt, Persia, Rumania, India, Australia and New Zealand.

"These six-wheelers scored a number of 'firsts', including being the first six-wheelers to cross the Andes and the first ever wheeled vehicles to successfully negotiate the Kalahari Desert...."

Several notable persons used Morris-Commercial 'D' type Six-Wheelers, including the late Duke of Windsor who, as Prince of Wales, used two on a hunting expedition in Africa in 1930. Harry Edwards describes the vehicles in his article:

".....One, a closed caravan, was well appointed and completely mosquito-proof, fitted out for use as dining room, bedroom, kitchen or bathroom. The shower bath was an ingenious affair consisting of a square zinc sump with a rubber bath mat in its middle and a drain to one side. Above, in the roof of the vehicle, was the nozzle connected to a water tank and pressurized by air from the engine-driven pump. Rubberised curtains slung from hooks completed the mobile bathroom installation.

"The second of the two vehicles was an open car used, literally, as a shooting brake and had gun boxes fitted over the rear wheel arches."

The 1930 Morris-Commercial Six-Wheeler of this chapter has neither overseas nor military connections. Its existence has been home-based, hard working and civilian. The chassis was purchased new in 1930 by Harold A. Barham of Wadhurst, Sussex, who bought it from Morris agents in Tunbridge, and had an open truck body and canvas hood made and fitted by a small firm near Paddock Wood. The Six-Wheeler was then licensed PN 7695 and put to work in the Barham Woodlands at Wadhurst.

PN 7695 was also used to transport the Wadhurst Scouts. Mr Barham ran the local troop and his Morris-Commercial carried Scouts to many events, in particular, to their annual camp on the Isle of Wight. A trip in the sturdy 'D' type was greatly enjoyed by the Scouts as, indeed, it was by Harold Barham's son, David, who still has vivid recollections of the vehicle. In a letter written in 1978 he said that his memories go back to "1930 or thereabouts" when he was a young boy and the lorry was at work in the woodlands at Wadhurst. He went on to say:

> "The land there is incredibly steep and the greatest excitement of my life was to go out with my father bringing back cordwood and experiencing the extraordinary ability of the lorry to climb very steep hills, sometimes using the tracks for extra grip."

> (Note: When not in use the tracks were rolled up and stowed on the running boards with fittings to hold them in place).

When Harold Barham left Wadhurst in 1933-4 the Morris-Commercial moved to the Barham family estate at Hole Park, Rolvenden, Kent, and ownership was transferred to Barham Estates Limited. Mr Barham was, however, still involved with the vehicle, and he says that it was kept hard at work until it was taken off the road at the outbreak of World War II.

Happily, this was not the end of PN 7695 as Harold Barham explained in a recent letter:

> "After the War we scrapped the old body which was very battered, but retained the original cab, gave the chassis a thorough check over and repaint, and had a new truck body built on by a firm at Benenden who built farm trailers."

PLATE 22—1930 Morris-Commercial Six-Wheeler
Photo: Edwin Bampton

Owner: George Budd

PLATE 23—1930 Super-Sentinel Steam Wagon

Owner and Photo: H.M.S. Sultan, the Royal Naval Marine Engineering School

1930 Morris Commercial Six-Wheeler 'D' Type

PN 7695 was re-licensed in 1946 and was once again used for heavy work on the estate and farm at Hole Park, Rolvenden. At this period the vehicle came under the care of Mr Charles Guy. Mr Guy had been Harold Barham's chauffeur until the outbreak of war, and when he was demobbed in 1946 he became responsible for the maintenance of the Barham Estate vehicles.

When discussing his work on PN 7695, Charles Guy mentioned a number of points; for example, he said that the cab seat was originally in one piece, but had been made into two sections at sometime before the 1940's. He explained that when the original magneto was beyond repair he had fitted a Fordson tractor type, and he described the flat-bed truck body that was fitted in 1946. Finally, he said that there were thought to be 90 grease nipples in the transmission and suspension but he had not counted them!

Keeping this 1930 Morris-Commercial in road-worthy condition was satisfying work, as was driving it, and the following extract from a letter written by Mr Guy in April, 1978 shows that he became accustomed to the vehicle's singular features:

> "When the lorry was loaded with oak cordwood and homeward-bound I would have to pass through gateways that had to be kept closed for cattle. So in low gear and lowest reduction gear I would jump out about 10 yards before a gate, walk forward and open it, wait for the Morris to pass through, close gate, catch up lorry and drive on to the next gate."

The Morris-Commercial was at work throughout the 1940's and was still 'going strong' in the 1950's. Mr David Barham said that it was used every year for "collecting hop-pickers and their families from their

101

Rare and Interesting Commercial Vehicles

homes in London and bringing them down on their annual visit to the Rolvenden hop gardens, complete with their customary furniture and belongings''. So it is likely that there are still families who remember cheerful journeys in PN 7695.

Ownership of this stalwart old lorry was transferred to another Barham Company—D. E. Berhams Limited in the early 1950's when Mr Harold Barham's father died, and there was a further change in 1959 when the log book was registered in the name of Hole Park Farms.

Almost three decades of work for one family company and its associates is a good record, and Harold Barham has pleasant memories of the lorry. In 1978, he told me how he had driven it across country and through the woods in earlier years, and said: ''....it was quite incredible where it would go, with the tracks on and in low ratio it was unstoppable''. Mr Barham never regretted his purchase of PN 7695 in 1903, but so many years of work in rough country would take their toll of any vehicle, and in the early 1960's Hole Park Farms sold the aged 'D' type to Messrs Ripley, Scrap Merchant of Hurstmonceux, Sussex.

Gerald Standen of Hadlow Down, Sussex, saw the 32-year-old Morris-Commercial in Ripley's Scrap Yard and made an offer for it. This was accepted, and Mr Standen bought the vehicle on the 17th October, 1962, with the intention of restoration; but he never had time to begin the work, and in 1963 he sold it to George Budd, also of Hadlow Down. If Mr Budd had not been a resident of Hadlow Down the transaction might never have taken place, for Gerald Standen found it something of a wrench to part with the ancient lorry, and he said that the fact that he ''would still be able to see it in the village'' influenced his decision to sell.

George Budd works with motor vehicles and he was

not overwhelmed by the prospect of the restoration, although he saw that it would be extensive. He explained that the lorry had been kept in good repair at Rolvenden; but it was, nevertheless, old and worn, and a fair amount of re-building was necessary to return it to first-class condition. This Mr Budd intended to do and in the following months he spent every spare moment on the work. The engine was stripped, the flat body on the back was re-built, brake system was overhauled, gearbox checked and new tyres fitted.

The work went well, and by the spring of 1964 George Budd began to feel that it might be possible to have his Six-Wheeler ready for the Historic Commercial Vehicle Club's London to Brighton Run in May of that year. It would be a tight schedule — but he entered the vehicle. As soon as this step was taken Mr Budd noticed that the date of the event began to draw nearer with remarkable rapidity, and he and his wife were painting the wheels of the lorry in their kitchen on the eve of the Run. When he set off from London to Brighton his 'D' type consisted of chassis, wheels and cab. There were pieces of hardboard over the wings and the bodywork was in alumunium-coloured undercoat.

Despite its somewhat unfinished appearance, PN 7695 completed the Run in good order and George Budd then decided to reinstate the vehicle's original body. He was about to begin the work when he received an exciting invitation to take part in a big parade of military-type vehicles to be held at Aldershot in the summer of 1964. This historic event was organised to mark the inauguration of the Royal Corps of Transport, and vehicles dating from 1914 to the present day were paraded. It was a truly memorable occasion and George Budd has always been glad that he was able to take part.

The Six-Wheeler had two or three other engagements after Aldershot, and the autumn of 1964 arrived before its owner could start work on the replica of the original body. When Mr Budd entered the lorry in the 1965 H.C.V.C. London-Brighton the body was complete with the exception of the canvas tilt, and this was made and fitted in time for the 1966 Run. George Budd's Morris-Commercial Six-Wheeler 'D' type has subsequently taken part in many London to Brighton Runs and it took first place in the Military Vehicle Section in 1969.

Fourteen years have passed since the rebuilding of PN 7695 and Mr and Mrs Budd have driven it to many rallies and shows held for charity. George Budd told me that they attend "as many of these events as possible between May and September each year". In this way the aged lorry is helping some charity in its never-ending search for funds and, at the same time, is creating interest in the development of commercial road vehicles of the late 1920's — a period of signicant progress.

The Morris Register lists five restored 'D' type 6x4 Morris-Commercial Six-Wheelers and George Budd's is one of these. It is one of the few survivors of a model that was well thought of by many people in many places in the world.

Specification details are :

Engine	17.9 h.p. — side valve
Cylinders	Four
Bore	80 m.m.
Stroke	125 m.m.

Gearbox	Two. There is a 4-speed forward and reverse gearbox attached to the engine and an auxiliary gearbox with separate gear lever bolted to the rear.
Brakes	Rod operated hand and foot brakes. Expanding shoes in brake drums on all 4 rear wheels. Foot brake assisted by a vacuum servo owing to the extreme articulation of the rear axles relative to the chassis frame and to one another all the brake connections are taken to a common centre between the axles, about which they articulate.
Top Speed	25 m.p.h. today
Fuel	Petrol
Fuel consumption	10 m.p.g. today
Unladen weight	2 tons 7 cwt 56 lbs

Chapter Thirteen

1930 Super-Sentinel Steam Waggon
A Powerful Alternative

By 1930 the steam road vehicle had passed its heydey. Only about 3% of all goods vehicles on the roads were steam operated. Yet this 3% was important because it consisted, in the main, of vehicles of the heaviest type; of vehicles that were capable of transporting vast loads. Many of these magnificently robust wagons represented the pinnacle of steam-vehicle development — and many bore the name of Sentinel or Foden.

The 1930 Super-Sentinel featured here is a good example of this period and it provides an opportunity to look, just briefly, at a firm that played a major role in the development of steam goods vehicles. Alley & MacLlellan Limited had not thought of building road vehicles when it came into existence in the 1870's. Its first product was the 'Sentinel High Speed Steam Engine', and thousands were built in the Sentinel workshops at Polmadie, Glasgow. Sentinel engines were used for many purposes including generating electricity, and driving marine and industrial engines. They were sold worldwide and Alley & MacLlellan grew from year to year. By 1906, when the first Sentinel road vehicle was built, the Company employed almost one thousand men.

Alley & MacLlellan called its new product the Standard-Sentinel Waggon, and thereafter 'waggon' was spelt with two g's in all the firm's publications. The Sentinel vehicle was well built in keeping with the Company's established reputation for sound work-manship, and it made a good impression when it was launched at the annual Brewers' Exhibition. Yet, despite these advantages, it needed hard selling in 1906 when many firms were still using horses for haulage and were reluctant to change. Persuasion was essential, and the case for motorised haulage was set out in clear, well-founded terms in all Sentinel catalogues, beginning:

** "A 'Sentinel' 6-ton Steam Waggon will easily travel 40 miles per day on fair roads, carrying 10 tons all the time with a trailer. Reckoning loads of 10 tons on the outward journey and only 5 tons returning, this totals **300 ton-miles for the average day's work.** Three two-horse lorries at the very best can carry only 9 tons 30 miles per day, thus doing only 270 ton-miles a day when worked to the limit."

This was followed by a comparison in costs:

Cost of haulage by horses.

"Capital outlay:		£	s	d
3 two-horse lorries at £30 each	...	90	0	0
7 horses (one as spare) £60 each	...	420	0	0
6 sets of harness £7.10s each	...	45	0	0
		555	0	0

** This catalogue and relevant material was published in book form by EP Publishing Ltd.. in 1972 entitled "Sentinel Steam Waggons".

"Running costs per annum:		£	s	d
Interest on capital (4% on £555)	...	22	4	0
Depreciation at 15%	...	83	5	0
Fodder, bedding and shoeing (15/- per week per horse)	...	273	0	0
Repairs to lorries and harness	...	35	0	0
Stableman and 3 drivers at 25/- per week	...	260	0	0
Veterinary surgeon, insurance etc	...	21	0	0
Rent of stables, taxes and sundries	...	60	11	0
		755	0	0

Cost of haulage by steam waggon.

Capital outlay:

Purchase of vehicle	...	578	0	0

Running costs per annum:

	...	23	12	0
Interest on capital at 4%	...	73	15	0
Depreciation at 12½%				
Maintenance and repairs, average	...	50	0	0
per annum	...	48	0	0
Fuel, 80 tons gas coke at 12/-	...	10	0	0
Oil, waste and stores	...	15	0	0
Rent of Shed, Taxes, etc	...	148	4	0
Wages, Driver, 35/-; Loader 22/-	...	16	9	0
Licence, Insurance and Sundries				
		385	0	0''

PLATE 24— 1930 Super-Sentinel Steam Wagon at Sultan Steam Rally 1976
Owner and Photo: H.M.S. Sultan, the Royal Naval Marine Engineering School

PLATE 25—1932 Beardmore 'Hyper' Taxicab Near-side view

Owner and Photo: Vic Bignell

1930 Super-Sentinel Steam Waggon

Clearly, the case for the Sentinel 'steamers' was persuasive; and persuade it did. Within a few years the make was being used for a wide variety of haulage. Sentinel waggons carried coal, bricks and many other heavy materials. They were seen in the liveries of local authorities, co-operative societies and Government departments. The make was markedly popular with brewers; for example Greenall Whitley & Co., (Owner of the 1914 Dennis fire engine of chapter 3) had four 6-ton Sentinel steam waggons on the road in 1910.

By 1914 demand for Sentinel waggons had outgrown the works at Polmadie and new purpose-built factory buildings were erected in Shrewsbury. At the same time an adjacent housing estate for the workers was planned, and this became known as 'Sentinel Village' when it was completed after World War I.

The first Shrewsbury-built Sentinel waggon was ready for the road in the summer of 1915 and sales continued to grow. This thriving state of affairs was probably helped by the firm's attention to public relations. Alley & MacLlellan never forgot that good public relations are vital to a successful sales policy, and the formation of the Sentinel Drivers' Club was an example. All drivers and stokers of Sentinel waggons were eligible when the club was launched during World War I and membership reached 5,000 in five years.

Club members wore Sentinel badges and received regular copies of a magazine. This publication included "hints and advice of great value to Sentinel drivers", as well as "interesting and instructive accounts of doings of other Club members". The merits of Sentinel vehicles were featured in the magazine, and every member was told that his vehicle was "not merely a piece of mechanism", but "a real pal to be depended upon in all circumstances".

Rare and Interesting Commercial Vehicles

The qualities necessary for success as a Sentinel driver were also outlined in the magazine:

> "All he (Sentinel driver) needs is an average amount of commonsense, care, intelligence, and a keen interest in his job and pride in his vehicle."

An especially pleasant aspect of the Club was the camaraderie it created among members. Drivers of Sentinel waggons helped one another cn the road and exchanged useful tips on the whereabouts of sources of clean water. Obtaining sufficient water was always a problem for drivers of steam vehicles and unlikely means were sometimes employed. In the early 1900's for instance, horse troughs and suchlike receptacles were often found to be inexplicitly dry when their intended users sought refreshment. Farm ponds were another unofficial source of supply, and it was not unknown for a pond to be 'sucked dry' by a thirsty steam waggon — if the driver was prepared to risk the wrath of the farmer and his shot-gun.

The importance of good public relations was remembered when Sentinel Handbooks were produced. There were written in a friendly style that was somewhat reminiscent of a self-righteous aunt imparting high ideals by way of a cosy chat. In 1930 the owners of Super-Sentinels were provided with a Handbook that ran to 71 pages of useful information and advice, and began:

> "The success or otherwise of the vehicle which has just been placed in your hands rests with you — the driver. This may sound a very sweeping assertion to make, yet it is literally true."

1930 Super-Sentinel Steam Waggon

Details of the excellence of the workmanship and materials used in Sentinel vehicles came early in the Handbook, and these were coupled with the reassuring information that "....it (the Sentinel) will carry on under conditions which would put a less robust vehicle off the road".

When, a few pages later, the remote possibility of a breakdown was touched upon it was pointed out that "no piece of mechanism devised by man will stand for ever constant neglect and abuse, and a Sentinel Steam Waggon is no exception". Then followed recommendations designed to keep the vehicle in running order:

"Driver and fireman to come on duty 30 minutes before their engine is due to start, and thoroughly examine all parts, oil up, and attend to fire etc.

"Ater a day's run both to remain 30 minutes for another careful examination.

"The engine to be taken in charge by a cleaner and a lad who will clean every part thoroughly, keep in the boiler fire, and prepare everything for the next day's work.

"Each engine to have a 'shed day' once a week, when the boiler will be washed out and any repairs done."
(Saturday forenoon was suggested).

How often these sensible suggestions were carried out remains unknown; but Sentinel waggons must have been reliable and capable of hard work since they were popular for so many years. The Standard-Sentinel Waggon was, in fact, in production from 1906 until April 1923 when the new Super-Sentinel came on the market. Seventeen years of steady sales.

The Super-Sentinel waggon was an immediate success, and the vehicle of this chapter was supplied direct from the Sentinel Works to William Brown & Co. Ltd., timber importers and builders' merchants of Greyfriars Road, Ipswich. It became part of the William Brown fleet on 23rd December, 1930 and was registered DX 9048. In 1933 William Brown & Co. had the vehicle converted to pneumatic tyres and fitted with a 6-volt CAV lighting set.

Steam vehicles were popular with William Brown & Co., and the firm used them for heavy haulage for years. It did not abandon its steam fleet until the efficiency and convenience of diesel vehicles had been proven beyond doubt. Even then the exciting and friendly days of the big steam waggons were often recalled. But not, alas, today. Mr J. D. Kelly, the Company's Group Chief Engineer, said in January 1978 that the last of the firm's 'steamer' drivers had died, and he added "....so we don't even have access to stories of that era".

DX 9048 was in the William Brown fleet for some years, and was acquired by Mr C. Lambert, a collector of steam vehicles at Horsmonden, Kent, in the late 1930's.

It is not known if the lorry was in use during the Second World War and it was next heard of in 1956-7 when it was owned by Messrs J. W. Hardwick & Sons, scrap merchants of West Ewell, Surrey.

By this time the vehicle's condition had deteriorated as a result of many years of idleness. Its continued existence was in doubt until the Suez crisis. This surprising salvation was provided by the Wingham Engineering Company of Canterbury, Kent. The directors of Winghams, fearing that the Suez calamity would **bring about a shortage of diesel fuel, decided to 'be** prepared' by acquiring a steam lorry. They wanted a 'steamer' that could be renovated for service without a complete re-build and DX 9048 appeared to be suitable. Thus the 30-year-old waggon was once more 'in business'. Or so it seemed. But the supply of fuel did not dry up, and the Sentinel's useful role did not emerge. It was used only for shifting ballast between Wingham factories on odd occasions during the first eighteen months of the firm's ownership and was laid-up in 1959.

Once again the future of the 1930 Sentinel was in doubt, and it remained so until a director of Winghams mentioned the vehicle to Commander D. Borthwick of H.M.S. SULTAN, the Royal Naval Marine Engineering School at Gosport. Steam had been a prime mover in shipping for over 100 years and Commander Borthwick was interested in the old waggon. He felt that it would be an exciting acquisition since it would provide a recreational facility for people in SULTAN and, at the same time, would be a tangible reminder of the importance of steam.

The idea was good, and Commander Borthwick wasted no time in speculating over difficulties that might arise. He acted. Wingham Engineering was approached; and after discussion an agreement was made whereby the vehicle would go to H.M.S. SULTAN on semi-permanent loan without charge, provided it was maintained at no cost to Winghams.

Then came the problem of moving the 'steamer' to Gosport. It would not be easy and Commander Borthwick and his colleagues planned the operation with Naval thoroughness. A schedule was drawn up giving route directions and specifying locations where the waggon's hefty demands for water could be met— all being well. An estimate was made of the quantity of coal required, and the 'volunteers' who would collect the vehicle were briefed in the art of 'raising steam'. Seemingly every contingency had been provided for when the party set off.

In the event the journey from Canterbury to Gosport was not without incident and a light-hearted account of the trip was written by Lieutenant-Commander J. L. Lees, R.N., who was one of the party. This was subsequently published in the *Journal of Naval Engineering* and made exciting reading. J. L. Lees describes the first sight of the Sentinel and goes on to explain that the spotless white overalls worn by the members of the naval party were black by the time they had 'raised steam' for a trial run. He adds: "I do not recommend steam lorries to the fastidious".

It is evident that the oddities of driving a steam waggon were brought to light during the trial run and J. L. Lees goes into some detail, explaining, for instance, that the brakes were steam operated and "if you forgot to warm them through" there would be a delay of "at least ten long seconds before they jammed the rear wheels solid". This would be calamitous in an emergency, and the author points out that "if all else failed there was a hand brake — quite suitable for any passing giant who liked pulling levers".

Drawbacks notwithstanding, the party soon grasped the rudiments of driving the vehicle and, having loaded up with 30 cwts of coal, they set off for Gosport in good heart. They were cheerfully confident as the Sentinel puffed along the busy Kent roads at about 20 m.p.h. — on the level. It was something of a shock when they noticed that the old waggon's progress was presenting problems to other road users. J. L. Lees describes the scene with vivid detail:

"We accumulated behind us a queue of modern vehicles full of drivers with very ancient oaths and old-fashioned looks. The more aggressive ones were easily dealt with — a shovelful of slack with the funnel blower on full and the wind in the right direction produced very satisfying results . . . . . On hills, where her (the Sentinel) speed would drop to a sedate minimum of two miles per hour the procession of vehicles assumed proportions which even Mr Marples would have thought impressive. We felt on these occasions, very aloof and dignified as we sat high up in our cab while the Old Lady regally chuffed at the head, occasionally disgorging disdainful gouts of red coals into the road."

Fortunately the members of the Sentinel party were not deterred by strong comments from fellow motorists and steady progress was maintained.

It had been anticipated that the waggon's requirements for water might be difficult to satisfy, and this was so. Garages were, understandably, less than enthusiastic when the aged 'steamer' puffed on to the forecourt for a 'fill-up'. Lieutenant-Commander Lees explains:

"We discovered that modern garage owners required a certain amount of humouring before they would allow a vehicle which oozed flame and fire to fill up with 150 gallons of water while it stood over their underground petrol tanks."

One garage, however, was obliging and J.L. Lees says: " . . . . we had two hoses — one ran from the ladies lavatory, the other from the gents".

The journey had its alarming moments — even to the end. No fanfare heralded the Sentinel's arrival at SULTAN and the Leading Stoker on watch at the gate was reluctant to admit the vehicle and its soot-covered crew. In J.L. Lees's final works, "he very nearly was our only victim".

Today, the Sentinel is part of the scene at H.M.S. SULTAN and is in the charge of Lieutenant-Commander John Havill, R.N., who has been responsible for it since March 1976. He gave me details of the work that was necessary following the vehicle's arrival in 1960, and explained that the refurbishing involved stripping down the boiler and re-tubing. In addition the engine and running gear components were all refitted and much of the woodwork was renovated.

The lorry was ready for use in the spring of 1962 and it was soon attending events in the Gosport district such as fetes and school open days. But word of the attractive old 'steamer' travelled around quickly and by 1963 it was being driven to rallies and carnivals over a wider area. Within a few years SULTAN's exciting steam waggon was known throughout Hampshire and Dorset.

Therefore it was a shock when the Wingham Engineering Company wrote to H.M.S. SULTAN on 16th March, 1970, saying that it may be necessary for assets of the Company to be sold and these "would include the Sentinel". The letter, however, made it clear that a reasonable offer for the vehicle would receive "favourable consideration", and it added that the Board "feel this would be a happy way to resolve the problem". This view was shared by SULTAN and a fair figure was agreed without much difficulty. Ownership of the 1930 Sentinel was then transferred from Winghams to the Welfare Fund of H.M.S. SULTAN—the Ship's Company being in effect the true owners of the vehicle.

1930 Super-Sentinel Steam Waggon

A certain amount of refurbishing was required after the transfer. This was done during the winters of 1970/71/72 and included work on the boiler and repairs to cab and platform. The vehicle was then in first-class condition and its activities were many. Undeniably, the most successful event was the Historic Commercial Vehicle Club's London to Brighton Run in 1973 when, having started off with a load of coal sufficient for the journey, the old 'steamer' completed the route without mishap, and took first prize in the class for Steam Wagons and second in the Outright Concours d'Elegance.

Since 1973 the Sentinel has been admired whenever it has appeared in public. Its excellent condition is the result of an on-going operation, for there is always work to be done on the vehicle during the winter months and a full restoration was begun in the autumn of 1976. To completely restore a 6-ton Sentinel is a big task and it has involved the casting of new cylinders, pistons, crossheads, cylinder covers and a legion of other items. Lieutenant-Commander John Havill explained that the vehicle has been "taken apart almost literally to the last nut and bolt", and that work on the boiler is being carried out to the standard required by the Navy's Central Boiler Inspection Unit. He added that H.M.S. SULTAN will be happy to assist other Sentinel drivers with patterns of the various parts that have been cast during the restoration.

In total the Sentinel travels some 3,000 miles a year and is always driven. Lieutenant-Commander Havill emphasised this when he said: "It is a vehicle that demands to be driven; we do not intend that it shall become a static exhibit having to be towed from here to there". He went on: "It goes under its own steam or it doesn't go". This, in fact, is one of two essential rules governing the lorry's appearances. The other

Rare and Interesting Commercial Vehicles

being the decision that it never leaves SULTAN unless it is in perfect condition.

So this 6-ton Super-Sentinel Waggon is always an object of pride to the people in SULTAN, and of pleasure and interest to all those who see it in action.

SPECIFICATION

1930 Sentinel-Super Steam Waggon

Maker's Number	8393
Length	24 feet
Width	7 feet 5½ inches
Wheelbase	12 feet 4 inches
Track	6 feet 3½ inches
Working pressure	230 P.S.I.
Type of Engine	Twin cylinder double acting. Steam admission by poppet valves. Two forward speeds and reverse.
Cylinder Bore	6¾ inches
Piston Stroke	10 inches
Unladen Weight	6 tons
Pay Load — Trailer	4 — 6 tons
Water Tank Capacity	Main tank 170 gallons usable
Type of fuel	Coal — "Mardy cobbles"

1930 Super-Sentinel Steam Waggon

Fuel Consumption	About 8 miles to 1 cwt. of "Mardy cobbles" — less on other coals.
Water Consumption	8/10 gallons per mile (more in hilly districts).
Top Speed Today	25 m.p.h.
Body Type	Platform body with dropsides. (Carries original Board of Trade load plugs).

Perhaps SULTAN's steam waggon has particular significance because it represents a period of great change in the field of commercial vehicles. Not only was it purchased new at a time when steam lorries were on the way out, but it was also new in a period when, for the first time, major legislation was introduced to control the commercial vehicle industry. As mentioned in chapter seven, 1930 was the year of the mighty Road Traffic Act which controlled the licensing and operation of commercial passenger transport. This was followed by the Road and Rail Traffic Act, 1933, which introduced legislation to control the goods road haulage industry. Before this Act the carriage of goods by road was subject to few controls and there was disorder.

1930 also saw the introduction of the Highway Code, the first edition being published in 1931. It sold at 1d per copy and was smaller than the present-day edition. The 1978 Code, which costs 12p, measures 7" x 4½" and has 52 pages; whereas the 1931 issue measured 6¼" x 4" and had 21 pages. However it carried, in addition, four pages of advertisements for motoring products such as Exide batteries and Castrol motor oil. It is quite impossible to imagine anything so commercially-orientated as advertisements in the present *Highway Code*.

Rare and Interesting Commercial Vehicles

The advice given in the first Highway Code makes good sense today as it did in 1931. Consideration for others was an important theme throughout, and under a section headed 'General' it was stressed that "good manners and consideration for others are as desirable and much appreciated on the road as elsewhere". And it continued:

> "Bear in mind the difficulties of others and try not to add to them.

> "Keep on guard against the errors of others. Never take a risk in the hope or expectation that everyone else will do what is necessary to avoid the consequences of your rashness."

The *Highway Code* is just one section of the great Traffic Acts of the early 1930's — Acts that brought order out of chaos in the commercial vehicle road industry. It is also true that they, of necessity, destroyed much of the excitment and challenge that was synonymous with commercial vehicles in the early days.

Fortunately these days are recalled by the sight of a steam waggon — since steam vehicles seem to have a special affinity with the period.

Chapter Fourteen

1932 Beardmore 'Hyper' Taxicab
A 'Friendly' Londoner

To many of us the London taxicab has the appearance of a hybrid — i.e., of a cross between a commercial vehicle and a private car. Only on reflection can we see that it fits snugly into the commercial role. Purpose-built and specialised, it provides a livelihood for at least one person; it gives a service to the public that is not exactly matched by any other form of transport, and it fulfils a demand. The fact that the number of taxicabs on the streets of London often seems woefully inadequate to the visitor who watches one after another sail 'disdainfully' past his outstretched arm, is evidence of the demand for this form of commercial vehicle.

From its inception the London taxi has met a demand. The industry has never advertised itself or offered cut-price trips to create custom. The passengers were there. Strangely, it was the manufacturers who were slow to recognise the unique role of the taxicab and to build for it. Many taxis were built to modified passenger-car designs and Beardmore Motors Limited was one of the earliest companies to produce taxicabs that were designed specifically for the purpose.

The Beardmore Company was already highly regarded in the field of engineering when it produced its first taxicab. This vehicle came on to the market in 1919, and it proved so successful that the firm decided

to carry out an extensive survey of the requirements of
the cab industry. The results of this research were seen
in 1923 when the second Beardmore model was brought
out.

For some years thereafter Beardmore Motors was in
the forefront of taxicab production, and the Company's
expertise reached its pinnacle in the manufacture of the
'Hyper' model which was launched in May 1929. Like
its predecessors, the vehicle was built at Paisley,
Scotland and was marketed through the Beardmore
Taxicab Company Limited of Great Portland Street,
London. It sold at approximately £445., retail.

Many motoring publications high-lighted the Beardmore 'Hyper' during the spring of 1929 and much was
said about the new features on the model. These included brakes on all four wheels, unsplinterable glass
and 12-volt electric lighting. The four wheel braking
was an important addition, and this was emphasised in
the 6th May, 1929, issue of *'Motor Transport'*:

"The four wheel braking system is claimed to be the first to
be approved for cabs by Scotland Yard. The fact that the
Metropolitan licensing authorities have passed these brakes
should be sufficient as far as their efficacy and suitability
are concerned."

The *'Motor Transport'* article listed other advantages,
such as:

".... The speaking tube has been replaced by a Dictaphone
electrical apparatus, which is much more effective than the
old method. ... Best leather upholstery is employed, and the
body can be painted in either green, red or blue with black
mouldings and wings. The body is so mounted that its
removal from its chassis is a matter of minutes only."

1932 Beardmore 'Hyper' Taxicab

A taximeter lamp was another notable innovation on the 'Hyper'. This showed a blue light ahead when the cab was disengaged, and *'Motor Transport'* described it as "a good feature, this, when it becomes known". I am told that it was fitted between the meter and the driver, and was some two to three inches in height and about one and a half inches across. It produced a small blue light that shone through the windscreen while the cab was for hire, and could be switched off when a fare was picked up.

In 1933 the Beardmore Company brought out its Mark IV Paramount taxicab and production of the 'Hyper' came to an end. Since it was launched in 1929 the 'Hyper' model had lived up to the high standard of production and performance that had been expected of it, and its name was associated with the best in taxicab manufacture.

The 'Hyper' featured here was built in 1932 and its present owner believes it to be the only restored Beardmore taxicab of this model in existence. Regrettably, it has not been possible to trace the name of the owner (or owners) of the cab during its commercial life; but it is thought to have been in London throughout this period and to have been working until about 1951. Many taxis had to remain in service for longer than the official ten-year period because of the shortage of new vehicles during, and immediately after, World War II.

The registration number of this 'Hyper' is GW2700 and its first known owner is Mr. John Brooks of Sanderstead, Surrey, who acquired it in 1955. His ownership was brief; and in 1956 the vehicle was sold to Jonathan Ellis Manasseh of Campden Hill, London, whose period of ownership was likewise brief. Julian Wakefield-Herrington became the owner in 1957.

When Mr Herrington acquired the 'Hyper' it was still in fair condition — despite its 24 years. He drove it on several trips, the most impressive being a journey to Spain which the elderly taxi survived with nothing more than a few blisters on its roof. Nevertheless, the years were beginning to tell, and early in 1959 Julian Herrington came to the conclusion — with some reluctance — that the 'Hyper' was no longer the most effective form of personal transport for him.

He was just thinking about advertising the vehicle for sale when a would-be buyer materialised. Maurice Kanareck saw the old taxicab parked outside Mr Herrington's home in London N.W.3., and was captivated immediately. He contacted the owner at once, and within a few days had negotiated the purchase of GW 2700 for £50. On 2nd April, 1959 it was registered in his name.

Mr Kanareck says that the 'Hyper' came up to his expectations and that, after carrying out minor renovation and upholstery, he used it for about four years as daily transport from his home in London. In these years he had any number of memorable experiences with the vehicle including a fire under the driver's seat while parked in front of Selfridges. He gave me a lively description of the crowds of shoppers milling around waving and pointing at clouds of smoke coming from what was, as it happened, a very small fire.

The scene was even livelier when GW 2700 appeared in the film "Watch your Stern" with Hattie Jacques and on the two or three occasions when it was used in television programmes.

The 'Hyper' was in service for Maurice Kanareck's wedding and his wife christened it "the duchess". She soon became as enthusiastic about the old taxi as her husband was, despite the fact that she always had to travel in solitary state on the back seat. Mr Kanareck mentioned a winter trip to Manchester and said that at the vehicle's maximum speed of 50 m.p.h., it was "a long, lonely journey" for them both. Perhaps Mrs Kanareck had the best of it sitting on the rear seat muffed up in her husband's old Army great coat and clutching a hot water bottle.

In course of time the Kanareck's baby daughter was a passenger in the 'Hyper', and her parents found that a ride round the block with the child in her carry-cot on the back seat was an effective means of getting her off to sleep on nights when she was fractious.

Probably, the strangest of all Maurice Kanareck's experiences with the 'Hyper' occurred when he was waiting for his wife outside Russell Square Underground Station. An old lady came up to him and asked if she could have a talk with his vehicle. She explained that she often had pleasant chats with vehicles, although she found that Rolls-Royce and Bentleys were "off-hand and arrogant". The 'Hyper' apparently had no such failings since the elderly lady said it spoke to her in a "very friendly manner". About eighteen months after this incident Mr Kanareck came across a letter in a motoring magazine from someone who had just had a similar encounter with the same 'transport-telepathic' old lady.

Not all the happenings with GW 2700 were happy or unusual, and there was a terrible night when the vehicle was vandalised while parked outside the Kanareck's home. The damage was considerable and included slashed seats and hood. In addition, a mirror and the large brass radiator cap had been torn off and were missing. All the damage was repaired eventually, but it was many months before Maurice could find a replacement radiator cap, and it was while he was searching for this item that he saw another 'Hyper' in a garage in Battersea.

All that remained of this vehicle was the chassis and cab, even the head lamps were missing. However, the number-plate — GW2872 — was still there, and when Maurice Kanareck made enquiries of the Beardmore Company he was told that his 'Hyper' GW 2700 and this vehicle may have been sold together in 1932 to two brothers; but it was not posssible to confirm this. Nor was it possible to see GW 2872 again, for when Mr Kanareck returned to the area a couple of years later the garage had been demolished.

GW 2700 had to be taken off the road in 1966 when its crown wheel and pinion was damaged, and it was still out of action when Maurice Kanareck was about to go to Israel to help with the setting-up of a television channel there. He decided that he should dispose of the old taxicab, and he was influenced in this decision because he knew that Mr Ernest Quinton had wanted it for some time.

Ernie Quinton was chairman of a vintage car club, a committed admirer of elderly vehicles, and the owner of several. He was the right person for the 'Hyper' and was delighted to acquire it. The fact that the 36-year-old taxi was in need of complete renovation did not daunt him, but he decided to store it until his retirement when he would have time to do the work thoroughly.

It is a sad truism that plans, however well devised, do not always work out, and Ernie Quinton was not to see his retirement. When he knew that his time was short he sold all his old vehicles with the exception of the 'Hyper'. The aged taxicab was something special and he wanted his son to have it; but this plan also failed tragically, for Ernie Quinton's son was killed in an accident in America shortly after his father's death. In this situation Ernie Quinton's widow had no reason to keep the taxi and she was glad to sell it to her late husband's friend, Mr Vic Bignell, who became the owner in May 1974.

1932 Beardmore 'Hyper' Taxicab

Mr Bignell is responsible for the care of the Post Office Utility Vehicle featured in chapter 17 and his experience of elderly vehicles is considerable. He knew that the 'Hyper' was in need of extensive renovation and he wasted no time in getting down to the work. His ambition was entry in the Historic Commercial Vehicle Club's London to Brighton Run in May 1975; but, as frequently happens, work commitments and spare time occupations intervened and the day of the Run came and went without the 'Hyper' — which was disappointing to its owner as he had optimistically licensed the vehicle.

In the event, the restoration was substantial and took many hours. The work included repairs to the Ash framing, new sections in the steel panelling, repairs to upholstery and the making and fitting of a new hood. Vic Bignell explained that he stripped the engine, gearbox, and all mechanical parts "to the very last nut and bolt". He was fortunate to have a spare 'Hyper' gearbox and using the best of both boxes he was able to produce one good gearbox. The engine had to be rebuilt and Mr Bignell had part of this work done by a well-known engineering company.

When the renovation was complete GW 2700 began to lead the life of a minor 'celebrity' which it has enjoyed ever since. It has been driven to many rallies and shows, has operated as a 'bridal car' on several occasions, been seen in the film 'Agatha', and taken second place in its class in the London to Brighton Run —this last achievement having made up for its owner's disappointment in 1975. Vic intends that his 1932 taxicab will continue to be seen in action.

At 56 years of age — this 'duchess' has a future.

Specification details are:

Engine	12.8 h.p.
Cylinders	Four
Bore	72 m.m.
Stroke	120 m.m.
Gearbox	Four forward gears and reverse. No synchro-mesh. Right-hand change lever.
Brakes	Four wheel. Rod operated. Separate shoes in rear drums for handbrake.
Top speed today	Approximately 40 m.p.h. but no speedometer.
Fuel	Petrol — two star.
Fuel consumption	Approximately 25 m.p.g.

Details provided by V. Bignell.

When the 'Hyper' model was introduced in 1929 it was a step forward in the evolution of the taxicab. GW 2700 is, therefore, included in this volume, although its early history is unknown, because it represents this moment of progress and the firm responsible.

Chapter Fifteen

1934 Singer Nine Van
"Is it so small a thing?"
M. Arnold

The vehicle featured here is thought to be unique. Singer commercial vehicles were never built in large numbers, and it is believed that no more than seven or eight are still in existence. These are all that remain from the entire commercial range; and the owner of the 1934 vehicle of this chapter says that to his knowledge it is "the sole surviving Singer Nine van".

It is a small, practical vehicle, and in 1934 it was just right for Messrs S.B. Cole, gentlemen's outfitters and tailors of Regent Street, Swindon, who purchased it new. The firm had been established in Swindon, Wiltshire for many years, having begun life as Messrs C.Y. Fry in 1881, become Fry & Cole in 1890, and S.B. Cole by the end of the century. In 1934 the Company was well-known, steady and reliable, with customers who were — for the most part — gentlemen of worthy character and average means. With such a solid image it is not surprising that S.B. Cole's new delivery van was signwritten with subdued good taste — thereby bringing the firm's name and activities to the attention of the public without appearing to 'advertise'.

The van was registered WV 6506 and could, thereafter, be seen proceeding at moderate speed around Swindon and adjacent villages. It became a familiar sight, and Mr Ray Lea, who was employed by S.B. Cole in 1934, still has happy recollections of driving it. He was, in fact, the first person to drive the vehicle when it was new and he remembers using it to deliver orders to country districts. In recent conversation he agreed that the little 8.93 h.p. Singer was not really fast, but he pointed out that it was pleasant to drive and had a neat and business-like appearance.

Messrs S.B. Cole kept the Singer on the road for four years before selling it to Harry Kilminster & Co., general building contractors of William Street, Swindon in 1938. This firm was also well-known and respected in Swindon, but building contracting is somewhat different from gent's outfitting, and the change of ownership brought an element of 'rough and tumble' into the van's existence. Nevertheless it was always well maintained, and Mr J. Barnett, who was a foreman with Harry Kilminster & Co., has confirmed this. Mr Barnett often drove the vehicle when visiting sites, and he explained that it was also used for delivering materials and men to small painting and decorating jobs.

When Mr Barnett described the vehicle he said that it "handled well for vans in those days"; but he added that "the driving position was a bit cramped for tall drivers" and that the van "had a tendency to drop out of gear now and again if strained in second gear". These minor criticisms notwithstanding, Mr Barnett had no hesitation in saying that the Singer van gave good service. He could easily have added 'long service'; for the building contractors kept WV 6506 on the road throughout World War II and on into 1949, at which time ownership was transferred to Frederick Kilminster of Britannia Garages in Swindon — Frederick being Harry Kilminster's brother.

It might be assumed that a vehicle's useful life would come to an end after 15 years of work; but this was not so with WV 6506. The doughty little van was in commercial use for Frederick Kilminster until 1963

1934 Singer Nine Van

when it had been on the road continuously for almost 30 years.

In March 1978 Frederick Kilminster's grand-nephew, Thomas Kilminster, talked to me about the Singer. He referred to occasional shopping trips to Swindon in the van when he was a child — with Great Uncle Fred at the wheel, and Thomas and his dog and the shopping in the back. But time passes; by 1963 the Singer had been at work for 29 years and Frederick Kilminster decided that its working life had come to an end. Even so he was reluctant to dispose of the vehicle, and he had it laid up on wooden blocks in a corner of the garage. There it remained until 1968, generally out of sight — but never quite out of mind.

1968 was notable in that Thomas Kilminster attended a motor sport meeting where he saw an advertisement for a parade of historic vehicles, and he at once remembered that old Singer. He explained that the sight of the advertisement suddenly "rang a bell" and he began to wonder if Uncle Fred still owned the vehicle. There was only one way to find out, and on the following day Thomas visited his uncle at Britannia Garages and saw the van in the corner where it had been since 1963.

Strange to relate, Mr Frederick Kilminster had received an offer for the Singer only a week before and had felt that he could not part with it. However, when his nephew expressed a wish to buy the vehicle he agreed to let it go and the transaction was made without delay.

Thomas Kilminster said that as soon as the old van was dusted off it was seen to be in reasonable condition, and was still carrying its 1963 'C' licence disc on the windscreen. The paintwork was dull, tyres and running-boards needed re-newing, and there was plenty of cleaning and rust-removing to be done;

131

but Thomas emphasised that the van was "basically complete".

It was planned to paint the Singer in the livery it had worn with Harry Kilminster & Company: green body-work, black lettering and a yellow coachline. The new owner was well satisfied with the result when he drove the van to its first rally, and it was a nasty shock when he found that the engine was over-heating badly.

This was a set-back, but Mr Kilminster wasted no time on regrets. To use his own words, he immediately decided that "there was nothing for it but a complete engine re-build" and, what is more, he decided — somewhat apprehensively — to do the work himself. In the event there was no cause for apprehension; the work was well done and Thomas enjoyed doing it. Indeed, he said that he had even more pleasure from restoring the Singer than he subsequently had from driving it.

On stripping the engine Thomas Kilminster found that the front timing chains and camshaft were the only parts that had to be replaced. He expected that these would be difficult to obtain and was pleasantly surprised when he was able to buy them in Swindon. The supplier had held a Singer franchise in the days before Singer was purchased by Rootes Motors, and the items were found stowed away in the back of the stores department where they had been for many years.

The work on the engine was finished by 1970, and Thomas Kilminster then began to take the van to rallies. He described its performance as good; and said that "on the flat and with a fair wind" it had occasion-ally been known to reach 45 m.p.h., but he normally drove it at speeds of 20 to 25 m.p.h.

The Singer attended rallies and shows during summer months for about four years, and it was not unusual for the vehicle to be out every week-end. At

PLATE 26—1932 Beardmore 'Hyper' Taxicab Off-side view

Owner and Photo: Vic Bignell

PLATE 27—1934 Singer Nine Van

Owner: Laurence Shaw   Photo: Thomas Kilminster

this time, Mr Kilminster lived at his parents' home in Wanborough near Swindon where the van was garaged; but when he went to live and work in Bournemouth in 1974 he,unfortunately, had no room to park it, and the vehicle had to remain in store at Wanborough. This situation continued for three years and Thomas was concerned to see that the Singer was deteriorating. Restored vehicles need to be used, and he reluctantly came to the conclusion that he must advertise the van for sale.

His advertisement was seen by Mr Laurence Shaw of Woodhall Spa. Mr Shaw is an authority on historic vehicles and he was pleased to be able to purchase the Singer. When I asked him in the spring of 1978 why he wanted the van he explained that he was "building up a small collection of Singer vehicles covering a cross section of the models produced". He is especially delighted to acquire WV 6506 because he believes it to be "the sole surviving Singer Nine van".

Laurence Shaw has a little work to do on his Singer Nine van, and when this is finished he intends that the vehicle shall have an active life — which is an ideal objective.

WV 6506 has a history that is economic, homely, hard-working and dogged; and as such it is a perfect reflection of life in the early 1930's. It is good that it survives.

Specification details are:

Engine	8.93 h.p.
Number of cylinders	Four
Bore	60 mm
Stroke	86mm

Gearbox	3 forward gears and reverse.
Brakes	Foot — internal expanding shoes in drums on all four wheels, rod operated.
	Hand — operating on all wheels.
Maximum speed	45 m.p.h. in favourable conditions. Normally about 25 m.p.h.
Type of fuel	2-star petrol.
Consumption	Approximately 60 m.p.g. when travelling at 20 m.p.h.
Unladen weight	12¾ cwt.

Chapter Sixteen

1936 Dennis Fire Engine
In Hampshire's Service

The Dennis "Braidwood-Type Six-Cylinder Fire Engine" featured here has the distinction of being in good condition at 42 years of age, of having spent all these years in Hampshire, of being known throughout the County as 'Boris', and of achieving prominence as a fire appliance, a competition engine and an historic rallying vehicle. This long and varied career began on the 31st July, 1936 when Dennis Bros. supplied the vehicle direct to the Aldershot Fire Brigade.

The "Light Six-Cylinder Model" was one of the Dennis Company's most popular fire-fighting appliances, and the firm's catalogue pointed out that the vehicle's "light weight and high speed" made it ideal for "long-distance country work". Furthermore, the "large-section twin tyres" enabled it "to be taken over soft ground", and the turbine-type pump, which had a capacity of 500-600 gallons per minute, was capable of delivering water at very high pressures.

Page two of the Dennis catalogue for this model was headed "SPECIAL FEATURES" and began with the following paragraph:

> "Compared with the size of the machine, the engine is unusually powerful, having a swept volume of 6,126 c.c. Generous bearing surfaces are provided, and the oil passes through an external filter, two factors that point to a long and thoroughly dependable working life, as no high stresses are involved either by prolonged journeys made at high speed over difficult country, or by continuous-pumping jobs."

Rare and Interesting Commercial Vehicles.

This was followed by six paragraphs of additional "Special Features" and the section concluded:

"Details of Dennis constructional methods are so well known as to render further reference unnecessary — unless we add by way of indicating the regard in which experts hold our products, the number of Dennis Fire Engines ordered by the London County Council has now risen to 249."**

In case this was not sufficient encouragement, there followed a list of some 700 users of "Dennis Motor Fire Appliances". Purchasers in many towns in the United Kingdom were given as well as owners in locations on a world-wide scale. In fact, the number of users overseas was proof of a fine export sales achievement that many companies would be hard-pressed to emulate today. The countries listed included:

Australia.
Belgium.
Ceylon.
China.
Denmark.
Egypt.
France.
Gibraltar.
Greece.
India.
Japan.
Mesopotamia.
New Zealand.
Norway.
Persia.
Poland.
Portugal.

**A big increase since 1917 when there were 50 Dennis Fire Engines in London — see chapter three.

1936 Dennis Fire Engine
 Russia.
 Siam.
 South Africa.
 Spain.
 Sweden.
 Tasmania.
 West Indies.
 Zanzibar.

Clearly the Aldershot Fire Brigade was in good company when it acquired its Dennis fire engine in 1936.

The new appliance was registered BOR 316 and within a short time was known as 'Boris'. It was a colourful sight on the streets of Aldershot with its fresh red paint, gleaming brass fittings and 'Aldershot Fire Brigade' signwritten expertly in gold leaf on its panels; but it was a colourful sight that disappeared with the outbreak of the Second World War in 1939. In company with similar vehicles all over Britain BOR 316 was painted grey from top to bottom — relieved only by a 2″ band of white paint on the edges of wings so that other vehicles and pedestrians could just discern it in the blackout. This drab appearance was essential in wartime and foreshadowed the sombre years that were ahead.

In fact, the war years were hard for Boris. The vehicle was in use more and more as older appliances became worn out and could not be replaced quickly.

In 1941 legislation was introduced to bring all fire brigades into a National Fire Service and BOR 316 was transferred to this body; but apart from being called to attend fires outside of the Aldershot area occasionally, the change of ownership made little difference. Boris remained at the Aldershot Fire Station throughout the War and until 1952, by which time it had become part of the Hampshire County Fire Service as a result of another change in the organisation of the country's fire-fighting services.

During its 16 years at Aldershot BOR 316 attended many fires; but there is no dispute that the most severe occurred when R.E.M.E. Workshops were destroyed on Bonfire Night 1949. The blaze was tremendous and some 40 fire-fighting appliances were in use. Boris, however, was the first to arrive at the scene of the fire and was pumping unceasingly for 15 hours. A notable achievement.

Another incident in the working life of this 1936 Dennis fire engine is remembered because of the bitterly cold weather. Whenever firemen travelled to an incident with Boris the officer-in-charge sat with the driver in the open, and four firemen were seated on lockers on each side of the body of the vehicle. They too were in the open, and a firm grip on the brass hand-rail was all that saved them from falling off when the machine rushed through the streets to a fire. On this occasion, a freezing January night in the late 1940's, the men were turning out to a fire near Alton when they found that the hand-rails were covered with ice and too cold to hold on to. There was no time for delay; so while the vehicle was moving and an icy wind was blowing scurries of fallen snow into their faces, the firemen had to take off their belts, put these round the hand-rails and hang on to them. A grim prospect; but all part of a day's — or a night's — work to the crew of BOR 316, and just one incident among many during 16 years of fire-fighting duties.

16 years is a long time in the ever evolving world of commercial road transport, and when BOR 316 was transferred to the Farnborough Station in 1952 it was no longer in the forefront of up-to-date fire-fighting equipment. Nevertheless the vehicle was still

1936 Dennis Fire Engine

serviceable; but it was not used while at Farnborough and after a few months was transferred to Alton where worse befell — since it was stored in a remote corner of the garages and left idle for about a year.

By 1954 it appeared that the 18-year-old vehicle's working life had come to an end; but events proved otherwise, and in 1955 it was sent to the Fire Station at Hythe and was in service once more. The log book for BOR 316 provides the information that it continued in use at Hythe until 1961 when it attended its last fire on 8th April, 1961 — this being a blaze at Lime Kiln Lane, Hythe.

Thereafter BOR 316 could be described as retired from operational work, although it continued to be stationed at Hythe and to have a useful role. Mr Bob Fleetwood of the Winchester Fire Station who is now responsible for the care of this vehicle, explained that it proved to be ideal for exercises — such as hose running races — at County Fire Service Competitions. These practical events were held more frequently in the 1960's when finance was easier than in present times, and the 1936 Dennis was often in use. It was also seen occasionally in shows and processions.

This was the vehicle's life until about 1967 when it became obvious that a thorough overhaul was necessary, and for this purpose it was moved from Hythe Fire Station to the Hampshire County Fire Brigade Workshops in Winchester. It was still there in 1970 when Bob Fleetwood noticed it at the back of the workshops. He was interested at once, despite the fact that the vehicle's tyres were flat and it was gathering dust as it slowly deteriorated. Mr Fleetwood thought that this was unfortunate. He told me that the Dennis "was old and nice to look at" and he felt sure that "people would be interested to see it" particularly as it was the "most elderly Hampshire appliance in

139

existence''.

All in all Bob Fleetwood decided that the 34-year-old fire engine ought to be seen at events again, and he asked for permission to ''have a go at cleaning the vehicle and getting it into running order''.

Permission was granted, and Bob began by cleaning the vehicle thoroughly and pumping up the tyres. Then he attempted to ''get the engine running'' and after some effort achieved this — but with disappointing results. Performance was poor and the engine was over-heating. This last factor was accounted for when the engine was stripped and the block was seen to be ''scaled-up'' to such an extent that the water channels were about half their original size. However, once this problem was identified it was soon dealt with, and the engine was running satisfactorily.

The next job was the bonnet which had been painted silver at some stage in the vehicle's working life. Fortunately a paint stripper soon removed the silver and revealed the original blued-steel finish which has henceforth been maintained in good condition with the use of an oily rag. The paint stripper also brought to light little brass flutes on the sides of the bonnet, and the vehicle's appearance was then in keeping with its elderly status. Certainly Mr Fleetwood was pleased with the result. He only regretted that he could not remove the chromium-plating that had been applied to the original brass work — such as hand-rails — early in the 1950's when polishing brass had become an unwanted occupation.

By 1971 BOR 316 was garaged at the Winchester Fire Station and Mr Fleetwood was driving it to charitable shows and suchlike events. He quickly adjusted to the vehicle's peculiarities such as the 'crash' gearbox with gears working in a manner contrary to the orthodox, and he almost always remembered when changing

PLATE 28—1936 Dennis 'Braidwood-Type' Fire Engine

Owner and Photo: Hampshire Fire Service

PLATE 29—1936 Post Office 30-Cwt Utility Vehicle before restoration

Owner and Photo: The Post Office

from first to second gear to count up to five between
disengaging first and pushing the clutch pedal in again
to engage second. He explained that if the gear does
not "go in on the first attempt" it is impossible to
engage it and "you just have to stop the vehicle and
start again." The pedal lay-out is also strange to
today's driver, with the accelerator situated between
clutch and brake.

Despite these oddities Bob enjoyed driving the
vehicle to rallies and shows during the early 1970's and
he specially remembers the National Fire Engine Rally
at Beaulieu which was one of the largest events attended. BOR 316 also appeared in the role of bridal transport which seems a somewhat incongruous use for it;
although on reflection the idea of a bevy of bridesmaids
sitting on the lockers on each side of the vehicle and
daintily gripping the hand-rails has a certain appeal.

In 1975 the elderly vehicle's social activities came to
an abrupt halt. Bob was about to take it to a rally in
the New Forest when he decided to make sure that the
petrol tank was full; which is a necessary precaution as
the vehicle only manages about three miles to a gallon
of petrol and is without a fuel gauge. Then he thought
"better check the oil as well", and plunged in the dip-
stick only to find it covered in "a horrible white foaming
froth". This was a nasty shock and it put an end to the
trip to the New Forest. Boris was taken off the road at
once, and investigation revealed that seals round the
bottom of the liners had perished and that the block
was cracked.

There was no doubt that a thorough mechanical overhaul was essential and permission was given for this to
be undertaken in the County Fire Service Workshops in
Winchester. It could, however, only be a spare time job
and progress was slow -- but steady -- until the
summer of 1976 when the intense heat and drought

Rare and Interesting Commercial Vehicles

brought many fires. In this situation the operational fire-fighting appliances were often in use all day and all night, and workshop facilities were stretched to the full to keep these vehicles on the road. Boris was covered with salvage sheets and pushed into the back of the workshop to await less hectic days.

Eventually the day arrived when the workshop manager, Mr Ray Board, decided that it would be possible to resume work on the old vehicle and progress was made whenever there was time to spare. 1977 with its ups and downs came and went and by mid March 1978 the work was finished.

A test run was the next decision, and this did not begin too well. The vehicle "belched up a vast quantity of black smoke", but this was its only sign of temperament. Within a few minutes it was running smoothly and has been doing so ever since. Indeed, Bob Fleetwood said that BOR 316 performs better today than it did in the early 1970's. Its engine is big and strong; it is as original and it is not worn out.

Since March 1978 Boris has been seen — by permission of the Chief Fire Officer, Mr. George Clarke — on several occasions. It has been driven in processions around the ancient streets of Winchester and to a variety of shows and rallies. It has taken part in celebrations to mark the centenary of the Victoria Park in Portsmouth. The Fire Brigade was one of the official bodies at the opening of the Park in 1878 — hence the request for the elderly Dennis.

The journey to Portsmouth included some miles on the motorway M27 and Bob Fleetwood said that he was able to "cruise along quite happily at about 50 m.p.h.". He added: "the engine felt capable of greater speed, but I did not wish to push it". Which is an excellent recommendation for a commercial vehicle that is past its fortieth birthday.

142

1936 Dennis Fire Engine

Specification details are:

Engine	8 litre.
Cylinders	Six
Bore	100 m.m.
Stroke	130 m.m.
Gearbox	Four-speed and reverse. No synchro-mesh
Brakes	Hydraulic on all wheels, servo assisted. Handbrake on rear wheels.
Max. m.p.h. today	Unknown — possibly 60-70 m.p.h.
Fuel	Petrol (tank capacity 20 galls).
Fuel consumption	3 to 4 m.p.g.
Seating capacity	Six
Unladen weight	4 ton 15 cwt.

Provided by B. Fleetwood.

Chapter Seventeen

1936 Post Office 30-cwt Utility Vehicle
A Workshop on Wheels

Post Office Linesman's 30-cwt Utility Vehicles were a familiar sight in the British street scene for a quarter of a century, and more than 1,300 were built. They were not the first type of motor vehicle to be used by telephone linesmen but they were the first to be designed specifically for them.

In 1916 the Post office Engineering Department borrowed a number of Army lorries, and these were the Department's first experience of motor transport. Prior to that time telephone engineers travelled to and from jobs by train or on foot, as an article in the April 1938 issue of the *Post Office Electrical Engineers' Journal* makes clear:

> "One can imagine the feelings of Post Office gangs 20 or 30 years ago, when they had to travel to their work by slow and uncomfortable trains, and when the final stage of the journey often meant pushing a heavily-laden handcart for several miles. It was not until 1916 that the Post Office Engineering Department adopted a method of reducing the enormous expenditure of man power in getting to the job. In that year Army lorries were borrowed for work on the restoration of open lines damaged by the great snowstorm, and they showed so plainly the advantages to be gained from the conveyance of gangs direct from their headquarters to the site of the work, that their use on a large scale was decided upon."

144

PLATE 30—1936 Post Office 30-Cwt Utility Vehicle after restoration

Owner and Photo: The Post Office

PLATE 31—1903 Electric Tramcar pausing between journeys at Crich Tramway
Museum—summer 1978

Owner and Photo: The Tramway Museum Society

1936 Post Office 30-cwt Utility Vehicle

Thereafter the Engineering Department's use of motorised transport grew steadily, and by 1925 the Department had 950 vehicles on the road of which 736 were motor cycle combinations. But none of these vehicles was ideal for the gangs of linesmen who often worked some miles from their base and were obliged to carry heavy cable drums and much other material. The need for a strong purpose-built vehicle was urgent, and in 1925 a prototype Utility was built and used for a trial period at Loughborough. This proved successful and was the forerunner of the 30-cwt Utility—the linesmen's 'workshop on wheels'.

The advantages of the new Utility were plain to see and by the end of 1925 there were six in service. Another 12 were manufactured in the following year and the model continued in production until 1938, by which time over 1,300 had been built. A proportion of these vehicles remained in service until 1950, and had it not been for the War it is likely that an even greater number would have been produced.

Many 30-cwt Utilities were built on chassis manufactured by Albion Motors Limited, the renowned Glaswegian company whose work lived up to its motto "Sure as the Sunrise" which was depicted by an embossed sunray motif on every Albion radiator. The sturdy bodies were produced to elaborate Post Office specifications by several notable coachbuilding firms, and were all painted in a pleasant shade of green, officially described as "mid-bronze green".

There was seating for the driver and one other (usually the foreman) in the cab, and for two or three men in the body of the vehicle. Considerable locker space was provided to store all the tools and materials hitherto carried in the handcart, and to make sure that these items were always returned to their proper places a plan showing the tools in position was fixed to the back of every locker. Insulators were kept in place by wooden pegs built into shelves; and ladders and telegraph poles were carried, the latter protruding through a small opening above the cab on the front of the body, while the other end of the pole was supported in a metal sling at the rear of the vehicle.

These practical vehicles were fitted with a small folding writing-table with convenient electic light on the left of the gangway where the foreman dealt with his paperwork — a vital part of the job. Space was also available for an 'official' bicycle, hence item 23 of the Post Office Engineering Department's specification:

> "CARRIAGE OF CYCLE — Occasionally it may be necessary for the fitter to stay behind and complete a fitting job and, in such circumstances, an official bicycle may be taken and put inside the body of the vehicle."

The 30-cwt Utility looked solid and sensible. Its distinctive Albion radiator with the 'rays of the sun' trade-mark added interest, as did the two sets of lamps — electric and oil — which were always fitted so that oil lighting could be used to avoid running down the battery when the crew worked for long periods in the dark.

There is no doubt that this vehicle helped to improve the telephone service to subscribers, and the fact is emphasised in Post Office publications of the period. The following brief extract reproduced from Post Office Green Papers Number 25 (1936) with permission of the Post Office is an example:

1936 Post Office 30-cwt Utility Vehicle

"...........It takes men quickly to their working point and brings them back to their headquarters, conserving their energy for effective work, and reducing ineffective time to a minimum. When not actually driving, the driver becomes a workman too."

On the contribution made by motor transport in general the Green paper adds:

"...........every vehicle put on the road carried with it a financial saving......."

And later:

"...........during the period 1931-35 the percentage of new telephone installations completed within one week from the issue of the advice note increased from 42 per cent to 85 per cent. This remarkable speed-up in the provision of telephones in every town and village of the country would have been impossible without the aid of motor transport."

Certainly the introduction of the 30-cwt Utility model helped to 'speed-up' the provision of telephones to subscribers, and the appearance of these sturdy, slightly top-heavy, vehicles soon became a familiar indication that the GPO was at work. Yet they have long since disappeared, and no other Telecommunications vehicle has become so associated with the service. Therefore it is good that a 30-cwt Utility has been found and restored to first-class condition in Post Office Workshops.

This is the vehicle featured here — a 40-year-old veteran. It was ordered by the Post Office in 1935, registered on 18th May, 1936 as CXN 247 and given fleet number U8068. Its Albion chassis was manufactured in October 1935 and bought for £303 5s. 6d. The complicated body was built by T. Harrington Ltd. of Hove, Sussex, and was produced in "best quality oak, ash and aluminium" for £143 0s. 0d. This price seems remarkably low for the amount of work and material involved, but as the firm was building two bodies of this type for the G.P.O. every five weeks, economies may have been possible. Both chassis and body carried a manufacturer's guarantee of 12 months.

CXN 247 went into service with the Telephone Manager in the Gloucester Area as soon as it was licensed, and remained in the same area throughout its working life of 14 years. These years were recalled when I met Mr Frederick Scull, foreman of the little gang of men who used the vehicle for a long period. Mr Scull was 77 years of age when we met in October 1975, but he remembered CXN 247 well and referred to it as a "very good vehicle". He spoke just as highly of the 30-cwt Albion Utility model in general, describing it as "absolutely marvellous". However, he was somewhat doubtful about the advantages of the folding writing-table and explained that he "didn't use it much" since it was "nearly always cluttered-up with tools and bits and pieces". Evidently paperwork was relegated to second place when it came to "getting on with the job".

Frederick Scull explained that 30-cwt Utilities were in use right through the Second World War and said that three rifles and ammunition were added to the complement of items carried during this period.

When the War ended in 1945 all the Utilities in use were becoming worn, for the youngest had been built in 1938. But they had to continue in service until the early 1950's, and CXN 247 was withdrawn in October 1950 having covered 87,700 miles. It was Post Office policy in 1950 to advertise and sell used vehicles by private tender to the highest bidder, and this 14-year-old Utility was sold for £90. 0s. 0d. to the owner of a saw-mill in the small Wiltshire village of Minety.

The new owner intended to remove the body and convert the vehicle into a flat truck for carrying logs, firewood and such like. But when he found that the cab was an integral part of the body, and that the body itself was more substantial than he had expected, he put the job off, stored the vehicle in a field at the back of the sawmill and forgot about it. Years passed, and it was 1966 when the old Utility came to notice again following an enquiry by Mr Victor Bignell, Transport Officer for the West London Telephone Area.

Mr Bignell was a member of an historic commercial vehicle club, and in 1966 he was looking for an old commercial of his own. He wanted an aged P.O. vehicle, preferably an Albion 30-cwt Utility which seemed to him to be "the most typical Post Office engineer's van", and when he found that the Post Office did not have such a vehicle he advertised in several magazines. In due course he heard from a man who had been on holiday in Wiltshire and while there had seen an old G.P.O. Utility in a paddock at Minety with 30 or 40 other ancient vehicles in various stages of decay.

On hearing this exciting news Victor Bignell went to Minety, saw the vehicle and met the son of the man who had purchased it in 1950. He made an offer at once but this was not accepted, and he then tried for some months to persuade the owner to sell. But to no avail, and he had given up all hope of acquiring the vehicle when he heard that Mr James Campbell White of Ramsbury in Wiltshire had purchased several vehicles from this dilapidated collection. An approach was made to Mr White who agreed to handle the transaction and the old 30-cwt Utility was finally purchased in 1970.

Rare and Interesting Commercial Vehicles

By this time Victor Bignell had an aged commercial vehicle of his own, and the Utility was bought by the Post Office Vehicle Club whose secretary at the time, Mr Ben Jenkins, still has vivid memories of "dragging it from its 20-year resting place in a field in Wiltshire". Despite the Utility's wretched appearance after so long in the open without turning a wheel, both Victor Bignell and Ben Jenkins recognised its value as a piece of industrial history and were glad to have found it.

The members of the Post Office Vehicle Club stored their new acquisition in the yard of a public house in Enfield for a few weeks, and then displayed it — still in ramshackle condition — at an open day organised by the Post Office Motor Transport Workshops at Yeading, Middlesex. The Utility was shown side by side with its modern counterpart, and looked such a sorry sight that the workshop manager, Mr Albert Hicks, declared "it would be a pity to leave the old vehicle in its decrepit state". He believed it was worth preserving, and in due course the vehicle was restored in the workshops at Yeading — much of the work being done by apprentices under skilled supervision.

While the restoration was proceeding CXN 247 became the property of the Post Office Corporation, and it was decided to enter it in the Historic Commercial Vehicle Club's London to Brighton Run in May 1971. The rebuilding was completed just three days before the event, leaving no time for a trial run; and when the vehicle set out for Brighton with Mr Bignell at the wheel, its only mileage since restoration was three times round the yard at Yeading. But it ran well and, after a stop in Croyden to adjust one of the brakes and another when the speedo cable broke, reached Brighton in good time.

Victor Bignell was accompanied on the trip by his

wife and Mr D.A. Roberts, Deputy General Manager — West London Telephone Area, with his wife. They all enjoyed the journey and were welcomed to Brighton by the General Manager of the Area who gave them a champagne breakfast on the pavement outside Telephone House.

This was the first of many trips for the old 'workshop on wheels', and at the time of writing it has completed seven seasons of rallying. It was 'runner-up' in its class in the 1974 London to Brighton Run and took the first prize in 1975. Another event of note occurred in August 1975 when the vehicle made the journey from London to Taunton without difficulty and was exhibited in the Taunton Telecomms Museum — an achievement that was high-lighted in the September issue of the South West Telecomms Courier.

When I saw the Utility in London during September 1975 it was painted in mid-bronze green, the once familiar Post Office Telecommunications livery, and was an impressive sight. This was also the opinion of Mr James Campbell White who came across the vehicle during a rally in Windsor Park in 1974. It was the first time he had seen the Utility since he negotiated the sale in 1970 and, to use his own words, he was "very impressed" with its appearance.

CXN 247 has been active in the years since 1975. The busiest year was undoubtedly 1977 when it attended functions organised by the General Managers of GPO telephone areas all over the country to mark the Royal Jubilee. In addition the vehicle took part in the filming of 'Hanover Street'. 1978 was equally notable when the aged Utility achieved first place in its class in the London to Brighton Run, and I have just heard (August 1978) that it is to form the nucleus of a collection of historic GPO vehicles now being assembled by the Post Office.

Rare and Interesting Commercial Vehicles

It is likely that this 40-year-old G.P.O. Linesman's Utility Vehicle will be seen at rallies and exhibitions for years to come, thereby giving many more people the opportunity to be "very impressed" by its well-preserved appearance. They will also appreciate that they are looking at a vehicle that is practical, strong, reliable, well-designed for the job it had to do and pleasing to look at — in fact, a perfect example of a *Commercial Vehicle.*

Specification details are:

Length	18 ft.
Width	6 ft 6 ins.
Height	9 ft 5 ins.
Engine	3390 c.c.
Cylinders	Four
Ignition	Coil
Clutch	Single drive plate with clutch brake to assist gear engagement.
Gearbox	Four forward speeds and reverse (no synchromesh).
Rear axle	Fully floating with overhead worm drive.
Brakes	Rear wheels only (servo assisted).
Fuel	Petrol
Fuel consumption	13 to 15 miles per gallon.

Chapter Eighteen

1903 Electric Tramcar
"Let it travel down the years."
Henry Burton

The heyday of the electric tramcar was brief, and if the motor bus had emerged a few years earlier it is possible that the day of the tram would never have dawned. But tramcars came; and as they hissed and clattered rhythmically along their tracks they made public transport a reality for many people. Indeed, there is a nostalgia about tramcars that is not matched by any other form of commercial road transport and they have always had a fascination for me — perhaps because as a young child a tram was the only form of road vehicle that I could travel in without feeling ill.

There were many reasons why I wished to include the life history of an electric tramcar in this volume, and I regretted that no suitable vehicle had come to light by the time the manuscript was sent to the publisher. So when Mr Brian King of the Tramway Museum at Crich told me, some weeks later, of a splendid 1903 tramcar, there was no doubt — it had to be fitted in. Hence the fact that a vehicle of 1903 vintage is featured in this final chapter.

By 1903 many electric tramway systems were established. In fact, the first electric tram-rail is thought to have been opened at North Fleet, Kent in 1889, and other British towns and cities were looking at similar projects. For example, in Swindon, Wiltshire an electric tramcar scheme was put before the Council in 1888 but was not accepted. Further schemes were discussed in following years and Swindon applied for a provisional Tramways Order in 1900.

Tramway systems were undoubtedly growing in popularity at the turn of the century, and Brian King, who is a volunteer member of the Tramway Museum Society and Secretary of the Tramway Sponsorship Organisation, explained that at that period tramcars "were not only the largest vehicles on the roads, but also by far the fastest". He added that "by night they were the most brilliantly lighted — often described as 'galleons of light' ".

The electric tram of this chapter arrived when tramways were 'on the crest of a wave'. It was acquired new by Southampton Corporation Tramways Department in 1903 and was thereafter known as car number 45. The manufacturer was Hurst Nelson & Company Limited of Motherwell — a firm that also manufactured railway wagons, and the truck section was built under licence to a design by J. G. Brill & Company of Philadelphia, U.S.A. Many readers will know that a tramcar has two principal components: a body and a truck. The latter item incorporates the traction motors, wheelsets and suspension system, and can be likened to the chassis of a motor vehicle.

The body of tramcar 45 was an open-top four-wheeler, with lower deck of three-bay construction fitted with longitudinal slatted wood seats. As with other cars in the Southampton Corporation fleet it was rather unusual in outline as its top deck did not extend over the platform and the dash panels were flat fronted. Futhermore the vehicle had a particularly 'squat' appearance because all tramcars operating in Southampton had to be built to a special "low-height" design. Passengers on the upper deck sat back-to-back on longitudinal seats mounted directly on the roof of

1903 Electric Tramcar

the lower deck, while the footwells encroached on the space above the heads of seated lower deck passengers.

Brian King said that this 'knife-board' style of seating was unusual in tramcars, but was essential in Southampton because "normal-height" double-deck tramcars were unable to pass through the Bargate. He pointed out that the Bargate was the main Norman gateway into the lower part of the city at the period, and he continued:

> "The overhead wires swept down majestically to pass through the archway, and notices at the head of each staircase read: WARNING BARGATE ARCH. PASSENGERS MUST BE SEATED WHILST THE CAR IS PASSING THROUGH BARGATE, AND MUST NOT TOUCH THE WIRE."

Details about Southampton's Tramway Service include the information that chimney sweeps were not allowed to bring bags of soot on board and fishmongers could not use the trams to carry their wares. Apart from these sensible limitations there were few restrictions and Southampton Tramways Department provided a popular and efficient service for residents of the city.

The wages of drivers and conductors of tramcars in the early 1900's appear meagre, but it is difficult to calculate their real value today. In Swindon, for instance, records for 1904 state that the commencing rate for conductors was 4½d per hour and the driver — designation motorman — received 6d an hour. A modest profit of £305 was made by the service in the year 1904-5.**

Most tramway systems were busy as the 1900's progressed and the vehicle featured here — Southampton car 45 — was no exception. It was in daily use and after three years of service was beginning to show

** "The Swindon Tramways" by L. J. Dalby. Published by The Oakwood Press.

signs of body wear. A thorough overhaul was thought necessary, and the tram was reconditioned and re-built to 4-bay construction (Mr King says that a careful examination of the lower saloon reveals evidence of this modification). Despite the extent of the renovation number 45 returned to service with the Southampton fleet before the end of 1906.

1906 was not, however, a happy year for Swindon Corporation Tramways Department. It was the year of the town's great tram disaster. In June 1906 the Bath and West and Southern Counties Show was held in Swindon and a tramcar — which was crowded with passengers standing both inside and on the top deck — lost control due to brake failure and ran away down Victoria Hill — a gradient of 1 in 14. The archives of the Swindon Divisional Library provide the information that the vehicle lurched from side to side as it travelled faster and faster down the hill. On reaching the bottom it struck the points, swayed and crashed over onto its side striking a horse-drawn cab as it fell.

A man who saw the tramcar crash to the ground was reported in the local press saying: ". . . . the passengers lay in a heap on the road, some dead and all more or less badly injured". He described the cries of the victims as "awful". Four passengers died on the day of the accident, one some weeks later, and thirty were injured.

When the immediate horror of the disaster had abated somewhat, it was found that the Corporation's third-party insurance was not adequate to cover the compensation required. Nevertheless, all compensation awards were met, the money being raised by an extra 1/- on the rate on the 1st October 1906 and a further 1/6 in 1907. Fortunately this catastrophe did not inhibit the Swindon Tramway Service which thereafter ran without incident until it closed on 11th

June, 1929.

This, however, is to look ahead. No such calamity entered the life of Southampton car 45, and the vehicle worked for many years after its return to service in 1906. It was sent back to the workshops for further alterations in the early days of World War I, and on that occasion the upper deck was extended over the platform to increase capacity from 48 to 56. This extension also provided partial protection from the elements for the driver who, having no windscreen, was exposed to all weathers in the driving position. It was not unknown for drivers of tramcars to work up to 12-hour shifts in freezing conditions and to muffle themselves in balaclava helmets, gauntlets, scarves, and even newspapers under their greatcoats.

Number 45 was in service for most of World War I, and as a result of war-time traffic and reduced maintenance it had to be taken off the road for a complete re-build in 1918. The vehicle was then in the workshops for about two years and was returned to service in what Mr King describes as ". . . . an experimental form featuring reverse staircases and front exit to facilitate passenger flow". In addition, it was fitted with a top cover which increased the comfort of upper-deck passengers, but drastically limited the routes that the vehicle could operate as it was no longer able to pass through the Bargate.

The elderly tram continued in service on limited routes until the Tramways Department removed the top-deck cover in 1929, thus allowing it to resume its previous attractive appearance and to negotiate the Bargate once more. By this time, however, the Corporation had a sufficient number of covered "low-height" tramcars for all routes and its few remaining open-top cars were allowed to work only at peak periods and on Workmen's Specials. This restriction applied to car

45, but there were still times when it was at work and loaded with passengers on both decks, as Brian King describes:

". . . top-deck passengers braved the bracing maritime breezes that swept accross Southampton Water. When the rains came they somehow contrived to cram into the lower saloon, later emerging to stand upstairs until the seats were dry.

"When passing through the Bargate, standing passengers bowed low."

How friendly this sounds. Yet the decline of tramway systems was rapid in the 1930's. The motor bus was becoming increasingly efficient and, what is more, it needed no permanent way of its own. Nevertheless, there were people who saw the modern tramcar as a useful and pleasant mode of transport, and in 1937 the Light Railway Transport League was established as a pressure group to support the retention and modernisation of tramway systems. To gain publicity the members of the League launched a series of visits to tramway undertakings and this policy continued until the outbreak of war in 1939. Even after 1939 a few members found it possible to make regular visits to Southampton which was not too distant, and where the tramway system offered an interesting variety of routes and rolling stock although it could no longer be described as progressive.

Southampton Corporation had, in fact, been buying a growing number of motor buses since 1931 and the first tramway replacement occurred in 1935. It was intended to replace the entire tramway system with motor buses as funds became available, but World War II made this impossible and the project remained almost as difficult in the era of austerity that followed the Peace. However, by the late 1940's the Corporation had to accept that both its tramcars and track were worn out, and since new buses were beginning to arrive at a steady rate, a farewell tour to say 'goodbye' to the tramway system was arranged for the 29th August, 1948.

The 29th was warm and sunny, and as an enclosed tramcar was provided for the commemorative trip the travellers were soon over-heated. When the vehicle reached the Portswood depot a deputation of perspiring passengers approached the driver to ask if one of the open top cars languishing at the back of the sheds could be used for the remainder of the journey. This request was granted, and Brian King explained that "in next to no time" car number 44 (a companion of 45) was produced, and he continued:

". . . its drab livery of wartime grey paint was ingrained with dirt, the seats were slatted wood, it was noisy and it lurched along, but in the summer sunshine it was a true delight!

"At the conclusion of the tour the participants were more than a little saddened, for they knew it was almost certainly the last time an open top tramcar would run in the South of England."

It was as a result of this trip that the members of the Light Railway Transport League decided to try to buy an old tram and preserve it for posterity. An appeal was published in the L.R.T.L. magazine and £55 was raised from almost one hundred contributions — some contributors being school-boys who donated their pocket money.

The next step was to acquire a suitable tramcar. A letter to the General Manager of the Southampton Corporation Transport Department produced the information that £10 was the scrap price for a body only; but that, in the circumstances, a complete tram would be available for this price. As the truck component is made of quality steel and copper and has a high scrap value this generous offer was accepted gratefully.

Southampton Corporation selected car 45 as being in the best condition and arranged for it to be fitted with the best truck in the depot. The vehicle was then sent to the paintshop where the oldest employee was instructed to use up all the tramcar paint — a process that provided number 45 with eight coats. This lavish repaint was not historically authentic but it served to protect the car effectively in the ups and downs of the years that followed.

The members of the L.R.T.L. had now achieved their ambition to own an old tramcar. The next question was what to do with it. Depot space was short in Southampton so the vehicle could not remain there, and the League itself was without premises. Enquiries were made and eventually space was found for 45 in the workshops of the Leeds Tramway Company. A Southampton road-haulier agreed to transport it the 240 miles to Leeds at an extremely low rate of 2/11d per mile, and the old tram reached its new home in good shape. Unfortunately it had barely settled in when parking space in the Leeds depot became short and the vehicle had to be moved on to Blackpool where longer-term accommodation was available.

Nine years passed while the tram was at Blackpool, and during these years it occasionally ventured out on special journeys. Of particular significance was the part it played in a small ceremony in 1955 to mark the transfer of ownership to the Tramway Museum Society. This came about because the members of the Light Railway Transport League, having acquired a number of other elderly tramcars, had become aware of a contradiction in aims; their prime objective being the modernisation of tramways rather than the

PLATE 32—Tram disaster at Swindon in 1906
Photo: By permission of Wiltshire Library and Museum Service

preservation of tramcars of a bygone era. Thus the Tramway Museum Society was founded in 1955 to take over and actively pursue the work of preservation.

The new Society found, to quote Brian King, that it had inherited a mixed bag of life-expired tramcars on the point of eviction from depots up and down the country. As there were no funds available for rented accommodation, the problem was formidable. It was overcome in the case of Southampton 45 and another homeless tramcar (Newcastle 102) in 1958 when Lord Montagu of Beaulieu agreed to display the two vehicles outside the entrance to the Motor Museum he was establishing at the time.

So number 45 came south again, and after receiving a coat of protective paint to minimise the effects of display in the open it remained at Beaulieu for, two years.

In 1959 the Museum Society was able to obtain premises of its own in a disused quarry in Derbyshire, and by the autumn of 1960 the members had erected some covered accommodation. Space was then available for car 45. In October of that year the Edwardian tramcar was transported on low-loader from Beaulieu to Derbyshire and negotiated the Bargate for the last time as it passed through Southampton on the way north. It was, at last, going to a permanent home, for the disused quarry had become the Crich Tramway Museum — albeit in somewhat rugged condition.

Since that time the members of the Society have worked voluntarily in their spare time to create the Museum. Today there are good buildings and workshop facilities, as well as a tramway on which 45 was the first car to carry passengers. Indeed, Brian King has said that the old tramcar was "the backbone of the public service while essential work was carried out to produce a functioning fleet." After some years, 45 itself was in need of a complete overhaul and this was begun in 1972, by which time the Museum had a well equipped workshop area complete with two tracks and inspection pits.

It was decided that car 45 should be restored to its 1929 condition with open top deck, and the first job was to separate body and truck. Thereafter the work was long and hard, and involved the removal of the two traction motors each weighing almost a ton. In addition, it was necessary to establish the 1929 livery, a job that was accomplished with the extensive use of wet-and-dry paper and 'elbow-grease'. First to be removed was the Beaulieu protective coat, followed by the eight coats applied in 1948, the war-time grey, and finally the maroon and cream that had been Southampton Corporation colours in the 1930's. Beneath these coats of many colours was found the 1929 livery, and on the lower side panels the wording "Southampton Corporation Tramways" in gold leaf. A tracing was made for future reference.

The restoration of car 45 took a long time and considerable expertise; but the day came when the vehicle was ready for repainting. Dash panels, staircases and waist panels were refinished in carminette (a shade similar to vermillion) and the remaining panels in ivory. Much other detailed painting was required as Brian King describes:

> "The carminette panels are lined out in gold leaf, and the waist panels bear ornate Greek Key motifs. The ivory panels are lined in a combination of sepia and light blue, while the lower saloon corner pillars are picked out in royal blue, lined in gold. The waist panels bear the full coat of arms of Southampton Corporation, and the rocker panels will be painted with the 'Southampton Corporation Tramways' legend in ornate shaded gold lettering immediately prior to varnishing."

1903 Electic Tramcar

An effort was made to complete the restoration of number 45 in time for the 1978 season, and after a programme of testing the vehicle re-entered service at Crich on Easter Monday '78. On that day there were ten tramcars in service at the Museum and they carried over seven thousand passengers.

45 is a favourite with visitors to the Museum, and following its return to service at Easter it continued in use until tramcar operation ceased for the year at the end of October. During the season it was not unusual for the old tram to work for up to eight hours in fine weather, and on occasions it covered as many as 40 miles in a day while taking visitors for trips on the museum's one-mile long tramway. When not in use Southampton 45 is parked in the main depot complex where it has the company of 30 other tramcars ranging from an 1873 mule car to a 1953 ultra-modern prototype that was never in production.

But, however distinguished the company, number 45 is special. It was the first tramcar to be preserved by enthusiasts in Britain, and its preservation led to the founding of the Tramway Museum Society and, in due course, to the establishment of the Museum at Crich. Southampton 45 is an important vehicle and, in a sense, it is as much a 'galleon of light' today as when it was new 75 years ago.

The specification details given below are provided by Mr. King, as is the description of driving tramcar 45 that follows:

Power unit	Power is derived from 2 x 25 h.p. electric motors. This is a nominal rating, based on the capability of the motor insulation to run at maximum rated output without over-heating. Power is transmitted by straight-cut spur gears.

Braking	Normal braking by hand-operated wneel tread brake, as in railway practice but without power assistance. Emergency braking by rheostatic method.
Maximum speed	Dependent on power supply. ɪ⋁υ speedometer fitted (or any other instruments), but approximately 25 m.p.h. on straight and level track.
Fuel	Electricity, 600 voits, direct current.
Seating capacity	As built — 48 (24 inside and 24 on top deck). At present — 56 (24 inside and 32 on top deck). With longitudinal seating, capacity is determined by the prevailing opinion of the length of seat required by an average-sized passenger. This can vary between undertakings.

Dimensions	Length of saloon	—	17'
	Length of platforms	—	5' 6"
	Length overall	— —	29'
	Width overall	— —	7'
	Wheelbase	— —	7'
	Gauge	— —	4' 8½"
	Weight	— —	7½ tons

1903 Electric Tramcar

Brian King sometimes drives Southampton 45 in service at the Museum, and it is evident from his following knowledgeable description that he enjoys the activity:

"The driver is obliged to stand to produce maximum braking effort, as there is no form of power assistance. Some tramway operators provided magnetic track brakes or air brakes, but in common with many older cars 45 uses a purely mechanical system for normal service braking. The brass brake handle is situated on the right hand side of the platform, and is applied by clockwise rotation. In addition to the effort required to stop the car, the driver has to overcome powerful release springs. A rachet is provided for parking purposes, and is also used during sustained braking, such as holding steady on a downhill gradient. Anybody driving a tramcar for the first time would find the handbrake difficult to use, as it requires a definite 'knack', but happily 45 is a light tram with a relatively modest maximum speed, and to an experienced driver it is very responsive.

"The controller is mounted to the driver's left hand side. It is a structure some three feet tall, two feet wide and one foot deep. The operating handle is mounted on the top. It cannot be used until a special key has been inserted and either "Forward" or "Reverse" selected. It is also protected by a switch/circuit breaker mounted on the underside of the platform canopy, above the driver's head. To start and accelerate the car, the controller handle is moved clockwise through eight graduated 'notches', one at a time, to progressively increase power transmitted to the motors. The power from the overhead wire is constant, and the controller therefore determines the proportion of power used, the remainder being sent to waste by heating a resistance situated beneath one of the staircases.

"The correct driving technique is to 'notch up' fairly briskly, in order to avoid overheating the resistance (easily done in stop/start conditions), and coasting once the desired speed is attained. If this is done too briskly, however, the driver will 'trip' the circuit breaker above his head, causing a vivid flash and a loud report. He must then 'throw off' before re-setting the breaker. Needless to say this should be avoided, especially when ascending a gradient, when the risk of over-loading the motors is greatest. Emergency braking is provided by rotating the handle anti-clockwise beyond the "Off" position to a further set of 'notches' which regulate the application of the rheostatic brake. This reverses the polarity of the motors, causing them to act as generators. The current thus produced is fed to the resistance, which is reluctant to accept such a current; thus the tramcar is retarded more rapidly than is possible with the handbrake. The electric brake is a dynamic brake, and therefore the faster the vehicle is moving the greater the braking effect is. As speed falls off a walking pace the rheostatic brake ceases to work adequately, and final retardation must be done on the handbrake.

"In order to prevent wheelslide under heavy braking in bad rail conditions, sand is carried in hoppers under the seats, being applied to the rails by using a foot pedal; it can also be used to prevent wheelspin when starting on hills. In addition to the sander, there are foot pedals for the warning gong and lifeguard tray reset.

"When driving a tramcar, braking distance is of paramount importance as the co-efficient of friction between steel wheels and rails is lower than that between rubber tyres and the road surface. It is, of course, impossible to take avoiding action in the case of an impending collision, but at Crich there is no motor traffic to contend with and no cyclists to get stuck in the rails! Care is necessary when negotiating pointwork, however; on the 'main line' points are sprung for normal traffic movements, but on the depot approach fan each one must be set in the required direction. In such situations the driver must also be mindful of the trolley pole, for this is where dewirements are most frequent. Speed must be reduced to walking pace for all pointwork, not only for safety but also to reduce strain on the tramcar suspension system and bodywork. The driver must also keep constant watch for any obstruction in the rail groove — these can cause a jolt at best, and possibly a derailment.

"To the passenger, 45 is well sprung but has a lively ride. On starting, backlash in the gears is manifested as a low-pitched growl, rising in pitch as the car accelerates; this is accompanied by the tread of the wheels on rail joints and the hiss of the trolley wheel, together with the kiss-and-smack as each overhead wire hanger is passed. At speed the rush of air on the top deck can be quite exhilarating, while the driver experiences a considerable sensation of power, akin to motorcycling."

GLOSSARY OF ANGLO - AMERICAN MOTORING TERMS

Throughout the script motoring terms are given in current English usage. Following is a list of the more frequently - used words whose meaning is different in American usage.

English	American
Bonnet	Hood
Boot	Trunk
Capacity of engine	Displacement
Carburettor	Carburetor
Engine	Motor
Dynamo	Generator
Epicyclic (gears)	Planetary (gears)
4-seater	Four-Passenger
Gearbox	Transmission
Hood	Top
Paraffin	Kerosene
Petrol	Gasoline/Fuel
Petrol tank	Gas tank
Side-valve	L-head
Track	Tread
Tyre	Tire
Windscreen	Windshield
Wing	Fender

INDEX

169

Index

Rare and Exciting Cars

DAPHNE BAMPTON

The biographies of 26 rare motor-cars are described in this book; cars that were young in the dawn of the motoring era and in the stately Edwardian age; cars from the 1920's — a great period in the development of motor transport — and vehicles of a more recent time. There are cars that have spent 40 or 50 years decaying in old sheds before being found and restored to their former elegance in a world that their original owners could never have imagined, and there are mighty racers from the days of Brooklands.

These are the vehicles whose biographies Daphne Bampton records with vivid detail. She relates the history of an exciting "horseless carriage" from the 1890's, and the disastrous adventures of a Vauxhall 30/98 in the Australian bush. The first car on Gozo is portrayed, and a Grand Prix Alfa Romeo that bears the legendary Scuderia Ferrari motif on its bonnet. There is the history of a perky cyclecar that still runs on wire and bobbin steering and of the Rolls - Royce Silver Ghost that once belonged to a great American Lady.

Brief engine specifications are given, but it is the social history of each vehicle that predominates, because this is a book for the general reader — a book for those who like cars, people and history, since all three are woven together in these pages.

ISBN 0 85475 118 1   *Illustrated.*

BRUNEL'S THREE SHIPS
BERNARD DUMPLETON & MURIEL MILLER

Few men have rightly earned the title of genius, but one must surely be Isambard Kingdom Brunel. In his short lifetime he pioneered the railways, built bridges, tunnels and termini. He also built three ships — the *Great Western*, *Great Britain* and *Great Eastern* — and each one contributed more to the development of maritime engineering than any other vessel built, either before or since.

With Brunel's enthusiasm for new ideas naval technology did not merely progress, it leapt forward with great strides. He piled innovation upon innovation into each design and defied and disproved accepted theories of the day.

This book tells the story of Brunel and his three ships, from the time that the *Great Western* developed from a dream to a reality until the present day. For the story is not yet finished. In 1970 the *Great Britain*, the only one of the three still surviving, was rescued from a windswept cove in the Falkland Islands and brought home to Britain. She is now being restored in Bristol, in the same dock in which she was built, and when the work is completed she will look exactly as she did in 1843.

ISBN 0 85475 093 2   Illustrated.

THE STORY OF THE PADDLE STEAMER
BERNARD DUMPLETON

The paddle-steamer holds a unique place in maritime history. When the early nineteenth century engineers experimented with steamboats they chose the paddle-wheel for propulsion.

Within twenty years the paddle-steamers were at work on inland waters and coastal passages. The first ocean-going steamships were paddlers. They were the link between sail and screw, a role they performed for nearly sixty years, and in shallow waters for over 150 years. Plying between the seaside piers they were as familiar to holiday-makers as Punch and Judy shows. In two World Wars they served honourably alongside the warships of the Royal Navy, and had their finest hour during the Dunkirk evacuation.

They were graceful, elegant ships, but in the jet-age too slow and uneconomical. In the 1950's they went to the breaker's yards in droves, and now there are only a few left. This book tells the story of the paddle-steamers, and of the men who built, owned and sailed in them.

ISBN 0 85475 057 6   Illustrated.

Published by COLIN VENTON LTD., The Uffington Press, High Street, MELKSHAM, Wiltshire, SN12 6LA.

HISTORY OF THE AMATEUR THEATRE

GEORGE TAYLOR

This book is the first to deal exclusively with the amateur theatre which has an important place in the cultural and social life of the community.

It traces its history from the birth of drama in Greece to the origins of amateur theatre in this country during the middle ages. Its development from the mystery plays of the trademen's guilds through the morality plays and interludes to the amateurs in Shakespeare's day.

The author shows how the raising of standards by dedicated individuals at the beginning of the twentieth century was followed by an amateur dramatic renaissance after World War I which continued until World War II during which the amateur theatre played its part in keeping up public morale.

Following the war, government and municipal support is noted with the development of theatre in education and the formation of civic theatres, the financial help through Regional Arts Association, and recognition by television and radio.

Illustrated with several unique and historic photographs.

ISBN 0 85475 125 4   Illustrated.

250 YEARS AFTER SIR CHRISTOPHER WREN
A. D. COBBAN

The Stuart Period in which Wren lived was eventful and saw the fall of Charles I and the Civil War, England ruled by a Lord Protector and the eventual Restoration.

During this time the art and science of building flourished under Wren the master. He was forty years of age before turning his talent to architecture and he was to spend the next fifty years designing and building. He was versatile and prolific as can be seen from his many designs.

This book is intended to highlight some of Wren's work of which St. Paul's, fifty-four of the City churches, and other secular buildings, remain as examples of his extraordinary talents.

ISBN 0 85475 089 4   Illustrated.

BLIGHTY

To soldiers in the trenches in 1914-18 Blighty seemed a comparative Paradise. But what was life in England really like in those momentous years? Many books have described the rigours and horrors of life at the battle fronts during those years but few have described life for the civilian keeping the home fires burning.

In this book we see the life of ordinary Britons during this shattering time. We see them adjusting to the bewildering changed conditions of life, wrestling with their problems in industrial and domestic life, and generally seeing it through. This in spite of the all too often loss of a near and dear one.

The young and middle-aged will find much to intrigue and enlighten them, while the over 60's with their own personal memories of those stirring times will find even more.

ISBN 0 85475 114 9   Illustrated.

Published by
VENTON EDUCATIONAL LTD., The Uffington Press,
High Street, MELKSHAM, Wiltshire, SN12 6LA